CAPTU
IN S

MW01045478

"Building a successful business in today's world is no easy feat. Capture Your Power gives you the sales roadmap to shorten your path to success. Mark Mirkovich shares powerful ways to help you become a sales expert. This is a brilliant strategy, as developing my own expertise in the mortgage industry helped me grow my business to 7- figure success!

CINDY ERTMAN
National Success Strategist - RPM Mortgage,
CEO & Founder - The Defining Difference

"Mark has been a friend and respected co-worker who rose to the top of a very competitive sales culture in a very competitive industry. His approach, shared in the pages here is an outline for any sales rep looking for an edge in their market. Mark reminds us that sales process does not need to be complex, but it does need to be planned. Successful sales process is methodical and smart. Mark's journey is in parts personal yet undeniably universal in detailing the steps to success for anyone in this business. These chapters contain the lessons of sales that all new reps need to read. Seasoned sales people are also to be reminded that perfecting the basics gives us the opportunity to polish and professionalize our approach to success"

JEFFREY WALLS
VP Channel Partners, FreedomPay Inc.

"We are all already selling! We are selling ourselves, selling our businesses, and selling our products every day! Capture your power in Sales and Business is a must read for everyone. The tips and tools provided lay an amazing foundation for all entrepreneurs."

DENISE WALSH
Black Diamond Leader - It Works! Global

CAPTURE
your
POWER
IN SALES & BUSINESS

CAPTURE *your* POWER

IN SALES & BUSINESS

MARK MIRKOVICH
FOREWORD BY PATTY AUBERY

PUBLISHING

Publishers Cataloging-in-Publication Data

Mirkovich, Mark, 1972–
    Capture Your Power: in sales and business / Mark Mirkovich.
    p. cm.
    ISBN: 978-1-7324703-0-9 (hardcover)
    [1. Inspiration & Personal Growth—Body, Mind & Spirit. 2. Sales
& Selling—Business & Economics. 3. Women In Business—Business &
Economics. 4. Small Business—Business & Economics.] I. Title.

                                                        2018908714

First Edition
Printed and Bound in the United States of America

Capture Your Power, LLC
20028 Grevillea Ave.
Torrance, CA 90503
www.captureyourpower.com

Editor: Nancy Butts | www.nancybutts.com
Design: Margaret Cogswell | www.margaretcogswell.com

To Julia, Jonah, and Jett,
You are my inspiration.

FOREWORD
BY PATTY AUBERY

Technology is constantly changing today, and that technology is pushing businesses to change and driving growth in every market. While times may be changing faster than ever before, Mark has refined tips, techniques, best practices, and insights that stand the test of time to catapult your success in sales and business.

I know first-hand what it takes to effectively drive sales in a global organization. Over the last 25 years I have helped build Chicken Soup for the Soul Enterprises, Inc with Jack Canfield. I started that journey as a secretary working on a door propped up on cinder blocks in a small apartment. Today, I'm President of Jack Canfield's companies, a New York Times Bestselling author, and a renowned business and strategy consultant working with some of the top performers and executives in the world.

As the chief developer, negotiator and strategist of Jack Canfield's career and companies, there has not been a negotiation, project, program, idea, opportunity, marketing plan or career move that I didn't conjure up or know intimately. Understanding how to position these projects and develop a sales strategy for each was absolutely essential to our success.

When we began our journey, we didn't have a book like this! We studied those who had already found success, worked with experts, and spent countless hours developing and refining our own strategies to hit our goals.

All of those skills came from 25 years of trial and error. Luckily, Mark has captured the skills and techniques business leaders have spent their lives developing. Mark's delivery of how to approach your business and sales efforts is not only extremely on point and effective but is easy to read and put into practice.

To your success-

Patty Aubery
President – Canfield Training Group
New York Times Bestseller

ACKNOWLEDGMENTS

I would like to thank the many mentors, coaches, and leaders who have taught and guided me over the years to think outside of the box and create my own path.

Thank you to my friends and colleagues Dan Harley, Kathleen Seeley, Jeffrey Walls, Chris Mirkovich, Jay Crider, Cindy Ertman, and Denise Walsh for previewing this book and providing your incredible feedback so that it could become the best work possible.

Thank you to Melissa Mirkovich-Scholes for giving me such an honest critique of my work. Your input helped me immensely on my journey! Thank you to Nancy Butts for your amazing job of editing this manuscript. I never knew how meticulous someone could be with grammar edits, but now I do!

Thank you to my mastermind groups for your support and guidance. I appreciate each and every one of you!

Thank you to my mentor Jack Canfield for helping me set the goal to accomplish my first book.

Finally, thank you to my wife Julia Mirkovich for always being my rock, my light, and my love.

TABLE OF CONTENTS

INTRODUCTION

Our world is changing. The pace of business has never been faster. In our attempt to find success, we are looking for new ways to do things that have not been done before. Our efforts are complemented by new technologies and advancements which enable us to learn more, see more, and understand with a greater capacity than ever before.

Although many things have changed over time, many others have stayed the same. Staples such as being organized, managing your time, and having a plan of action have maintained their importance year after year. But in today's environment, we are challenged to reinvent the things that we do and the ways that we do them.

Finding success today comes from dropping the same old clichéd sales pitches that may have worked in the past. Our approach needs to be more creative. Our work needs to be more efficient. Our resources need to be more abundant and our relationships need to be stronger. We are compelled to be more evolved, more open to unfamiliar ideas, and more accepting of new possibilities.

In the pages that follow, I have challenged the typical sales position and approach to sales by creating a new methodology. By using this material in my own career, I have achieved things

Introduction

that I never thought possible. I have broken sales records, climbed the ranks through multiple promotions, and created a life of abundance. I have achieved my goals and set new goals for what will come next, and with this new information, you can do the same.

I will show you how to identify your customer base, create a plan to penetrate your market, and introduce a new comprehensive sales process which will catapult you to success. Additionally, I will introduce proven methods of creating the best mindset so that you can take your sales to the next level. Together we will explore setting goals, learn to use the power of visualization, and create a daily routine to ensure that you are best prepared to engage your marketplace.

I wrote this book to help those who need a blueprint. I wanted to give clues of how to rise to the top in sales and business. This is intended for both newcomers and seasoned professionals. Most who are successful already have figured out some of what I have written here. If you are already there, then this book serves as a reminder of the basics that got you to where you are today. If you are not so lucky to be there yet, then let this serve as your guide. If you only do what is here, then you will be successful. Throw in some luck as well, and you can reach heights you never thought possible.

After you have read and implemented what you have learned, please share your success stories with me at Mark@ CaptureYourPower.com. I look forward to sharing your wins with you!

part 1

SETTING THE FOUNDATION

STARTING WITH THE END IN MIND

When I was a young boy at the age of eight, I attended a small elementary school called St. Charles in North Hollywood, California. The school had many fundraisers every year, and there was always plenty of competition that accompanied each event. The children, sometimes with the help of their parents, competed to raise the most money and win the prizes associated with the contest. It wasn't so much the prizes that drew people in, but rather the bragging rights that came along with winning the contest. There was the summer carnival ticket contest, the spring egg hunt contest, the Christmas boutique, and most important of all, the Thanksgiving turkey raffle contest.

The turkey raffle was pretty simple. Each child was asked to take a book of twenty tickets that they had to sell at $5 per ticket, making each book value $100. The child was to fill out both their name and grade on each ticket as well as write in the information of the person purchasing the ticket. The purchaser's information would then be used to contact the winner if that ticket was drawn in the raffle.

The contest was scheduled to start in early October and last thirty days so that all winners would be identified before

Thanksgiving. Each raffle winner would receive a 15-pound turkey from the local grocery store, and the child that sold the most tickets would receive a 20-pound turkey and be crowned the turkey raffle champion! Additionally, each participant's name would be posted in the school auditorium and a running tracker of the children's progress would also be next to it so that all could see who was in the lead over the thirty days.

Before the contest started, there was a lot of chatter in the schoolyard. It seemed that there was an eighth grader named Natalie Ruther from years back who had set the record for the most turkey raffle tickets sold. Natalie had sold 177 tickets, nearly nine books, and raised a total of $885 in thirty days. This was a feat that had never been challenged since. No one had even passed the $500 mark in all of the years before or after her efforts.

How could she sell so many tickets? How did she get through it? I imagined her writing out her name and the name of each and every person on each ticket. I was sure that her hand had blisters from holding the pencil for so long. There were even rumors that she broke a finger from overuse!

I wanted to beat this record and take the crown from her. I wanted this more than anything. I knew that if I was going to accomplish this, without breaking a finger or causing serious bodily injury, I would need a plan. I would also need help. And so my journey began …

I started to think about a plan for how I would win. I knew that I had a month to sell as many tickets as possible. After some quick math, I realized that if I wanted to beat Natalie I would need to sell at least six tickets a day, each day, for thirty days. This would give me a total of 180 tickets. Now, I thought that selling six tickets daily was a weird total to shoot for, so I thought that I should try to sell a round number of ten tickets a day. That way I could take a few days off as well and would not need to go and sell every day. I was a kid, you know, and I had other priorities like baseball, video games, and other very important eight-year-old things to do.

The one constant that drove me was the thought of winning the crown and being the champion. My goal of ten tickets a day would give me a total of 300 tickets sold at the end of thirty days and produce $1,500 in revenue. This would be a total that no one would ever be able to surpass. I had my goal in mind, I knew my timeline, and I had my incremental steps for daily action, but I needed a bit more prep as well. I needed to complete all of my ticket books with my name as I knew that this would save me time down the road. I started to fill in this information on each ticket the first night and had visions of Natalie Ruther doing the same thing as she prepped her tickets many years before. As the cramps in my fingers grew more intense, I wondered if there was another way to accomplish this. I then remembered that I had something that Natalie didn't, and I knew that I could use this to my advantage. Enter my family.

To offer a bit of backstory here, it is important to note that I am the youngest child in a family of twelve children. As you can imagine, this meant that there was always someone around to play with or yell at. I wondered if one of these able pairs of hands could help me fill in all the information that I needed to complete. I approached a few of my siblings and enlisted their help. What seemed to me to be my first daunting task of completing this information was knocked out in less than an hour. Additionally, one of my siblings suggested that I fill in the city, state, and zip code for a large number of the tickets as I would be going door to door in my neighborhood and this would save me time at each house. We completed this as a team and I felt ready to go the next day. I planned to come home right after school, grab my ticket books, and start selling. I was ready and excited to begin my path to the crown.

The following day I came home as planned, grabbed my books, and headed out. I marched down to the end of the driveway and looked left and right and up and down my street. I decided that I would go left first and start with my next-door neighbor, Mrs. Sweeny. I knocked on her door and she quickly answered and invited me in. I then began to tell her about the contest and her opportunity to win the turkey. I told her of my vision to win the crown and rise to greatness as the most accomplished ticket seller in St. Charles' history. I provided details about Natalie Ruther and her journey to greatness. Mrs. Sweeny was a great listener. She gave me water and ice cream as we talked and then invited me to the back yard to play with her dogs.

She had been our neighbor for over twenty years and was a close friend of our family. In fact, most of the neighborhood was very close and had been friends with our large family over the years. Each of my siblings had knocked on neighbor's doors at one time or another over the years, and most were very familiar with our family. Mrs. Sweeny agreed to purchase two tickets and gave me $10 in cash. I completed her ticket information for her, tore off the section that was meant for her to keep, and thanked her. As I left, I felt the power of my first sale. I felt unstoppable! What I did not realize was that I had spent almost an hour at Mrs. Sweeny's house and I only had about an hour left before I needed to be home for dinner. I moved to the next house and talked with Mrs. Henderson. She was a nice lady who had some older kids that used to play with my older brothers. Every time she saw me she would pull toys out of a box in her garage that were no longer used by her children. This time was no different. She quickly pulled me in to her garage, and we found a box of Legos that I played with for the next hour.

Once I heard my mom calling me for dinner, I realized that I had lost my chance to sell any more that day. Mrs. Henderson quickly bought two tickets and handed me a $10 bill. I raced home for dinner with a total of four tickets sold. I also got some ice cream and Legos to boot. Over dinner, I thought about my efforts and knew that I needed to stay more focused—and not become distracted by ice cream and Legos. I was short of my goal of ten tickets for the first day. I needed to stick to my plan and be aware of the distractions that would pull me off course. The next day I vowed to be ready and stay on target.

Over the next few days I found my groove. I knew that there would be possible distractions at every door. I told myself that I wouldn't stay at any house longer than ten minutes so that I could hit more houses. By the end of the week I had sold an average of five tickets a day, but I was still short of my target. I had already covered most of my immediate neighborhood, and there were many houses that I skipped as there was no one home when I knocked.

Starting With the End in Mind

I went to church on Sunday and had an epiphany as I exited the service that morning. I saw hundreds of people standing around after the service and thought, "These people all need raffle tickets, and I need to be the one to sell to them." I convinced my dad to run me home and bring me back to stand in front of the church for the rest of the day to sell tickets to anyone who walked by. By the end of that Sunday, I had sold nearly fifty tickets. I couldn't believe that I had sold that many. From that Sunday through the end of the competition, there were at least five other kids trying to sell tickets in front of church, before and after each service. I had been the first to do it and had capitalized on being the only one there on the first day, but others quickly took my idea and my future sales. There were even some kids that would hang out in the parking lots in an effort to catch people coming out of their cars first. The sales climate was getting fierce. My numbers were good, but I needed to work harder and smarter to win.

I spent the next few weeks revising my plan daily. I realized that if I could go to public places where there were more people I would have a greater chance of selling more tickets. I would hang out at the local grocery store and also make sure that I hit specific houses on the way there and back that I had missed previously. I started asking each purchaser if they had address labels so that I didn't have to write anything out. I asked my dad to take me to work with him on Saturdays so that I could try to sell to his customers and other businesses in the area. I went to the baseball field and tried to sell to people in the stands. I went everywhere I could to sell more and I didn't stop until the last day. I could taste the turkey and feel the crown on my head, and it was amazing.

At the conclusion of the contest I had sold a total of 297 tickets and brought in $1,485 in proceeds. Although I was three tickets shy of my goal, I was more than 150 tickets ahead of my closest competitor. Due to my efforts, I was recognized by my school principal in our auditorium during an assembly and was even mentioned by the pastor of my church during Sunday service.

The following week, I went with my dad to collect the big-winner's turkey and brought it home to my mom. I recall her two-day process of prepping the bird and all of the side dishes for our family Thanksgiving dinner. I can still remember sitting at the table with my entire family and eating that meal, with the centerpiece of it being the turkey that was provided by my hard work. I experienced feelings at that moment that I would try to replicate for a large part of my future. I loved to provide for my family. I felt pride for being the breadwinner (or turkey winner), and thankful to have my family's help and support throughout the contest. It truly was an event in my life that I will never forget.

As I look back at that contest, I cannot help but think about all the things that I learned through the process—things that I would use over and over throughout my life in many different situations, both personally and professionally. This was my first sales experience that I can remember, and the lessons that it taught me still ring true today. There are tools that I employed then that I have carried throughout my life to close deals both large and small, capture success in multiple industries, and maintain and strengthen relationships today. I have used these to rise to the top of multiple sales teams, break sales records that some thought could never be touched, reap financial rewards, earn the respect of my peers, build long-standing relationships, and create a life of fulfillment.

My goal in writing this book is to share with you what I have learned and provide these tools in a simple format so that you can use them at will, both professionally and personally. You see, these tools are not complex. They are simple fundamentals that can make anyone successful. They form the cornerstones on which you can build your success. You do not need a degree to learn how to use them. You do not need to be a certain age, ethnicity, or social class to reap the benefits of these. They are here for everybody. They are available today. They are within your reach. Now let's get started on your journey to success!

takeaways & key ideas

1. With the right tools, anyone can succeed in sales.
2. You have gained knowledge your entire life which, with proper application, can lead to success in sales and business.
3. At the heart of sales is your willingness to be yourself, seek for answers, lead with integrity, and help others solve problems.

considerations

1. Think about my story. Is there a similar experience in your life that engrained sales and business principles in you? What did you learn from this experience?

EVERYONE IS IN SALES

Typically, a sale is defined as a transaction in which goods are exchanged for money. Although this is the standard definition, there are other transactions which occur daily that are another kind of sale. Negotiating with your preteen daughter to ditch her cell phone for two hours to play games with the family is just this kind of intangible "sale." This broader notion of what a sale is leads to the recognition that such transactions occur all day, every day, in multiple scenarios. Regardless of whether or not you are consciously making a "sale," you are actually in sales.

In many organizations today, there are a number of different people and departments who impact the overall sales experience. As a salesperson, your responsibility may be to go out and find new customers to sell your products and services to. Your role is important as you are the one who is "selling the dream" of what your product or service can do. Although your role is a pivotal step in the process as it is the realization of revenue, it may only be one piece of the sales process.

If we peel back the onion, we recognize that you would not be able to sell the product or service had it not first been packaged and ready for public consumption. Furthermore, to be able to have it ready to package, there may have been multiple teams of people who helped prepare the final offering. Groups such as manufacturing, engineers, and developers are needed to produce, assemble, and map out the plan for the version of that product or service to hit the market. Once the offering is ready for the public, the marketing and promotional teams need to build a campaign to introduce it to the prospective customer base. You also may sell in an environment where an implementation or support team needs to be in place to get the customer up and running, and perhaps offer ongoing support. Additionally, the executive team needs to ensure that all of the various team's plans and actions are in harmony with the overall corporate strategic and financial direction.

At each of these steps, there may be interactions with existing customers, advisors, and user groups so that your organization can keep its finger on the pulse of what is needed in the marketplace. Each of these touch points are "sales calls" in a way. Each of these interactions can add to or detract from the overall experience of the user. Even in casual social engagements where an employee can discuss any of these topics with someone else, elements of a "sales call" are taking place. Additionally, I would argue that any other touch points that can influence the experience and perception of the marketplace can be added to the sales call category.

In this corporate or professional setting, it makes that sales would be the driving force to produce things such as product development, market saturation, and further organizational growth. But how does this apply in a personal setting? How are you "sales people" in everyday life? Let's start by reminding you again of what sales actually is.

A sale is any situation where the seller tries to persuade the buyer to agree to a specific action or outcome. In layman's terms, the salesperson wants you to see it their way or recognize value in their offer. They want you to "buy" what they are selling both figuratively and literally. The expression or act of the sale can come in many forms. It is this expression, or communication, of your desire or belief that is your "sales pitch," so to speak.

> **" *A sale is any situation where the seller tries to persuade the buyer to agree to a specific action or outcome.*

We can see this play out in many settings, whether it is a person at a bar trying to get the attention of another or a discussion about dinner options with your spouse. I recently had a conversation with my eleven-year-old son, Jonah, about a game that he wanted. His objective was to have me purchase a video game that he could download to his iPad. He knew the cost of the game ($19.99). He also knew that whenever he asked me for a new game, my first question would be, "Is this a free download?" He had obviously put some thought into how and when he would ask me in order to overcome my objections. He also knew that if he asked me in front of his mom he would have a better chance as apparently, I say "no" a lot, while his mom is a bit more patient in evaluating each request. He brought up the subject during a family dinner and the dialogue went something like this.

Jonah: Daddy, do you remember that commercial we saw for that football game on the iPad a few weeks ago?

Me: Yes (as I raised an eyebrow suspecting what was coming next).

Jonah: Do you remember how cool the graphics were? And it has all of the new rosters for all of the teams, even the Steelers. (He knows that the Steelers are my favorite team.)

Me: Yes, that's pretty cool.

Jonah: Well, they just released the game today and it's available for download.

Me: Really?

Jonah: Yeah—can I get it?

Me: Is it a free download? (knowing that it wasn't).

Jonah: It's free for you. (He smiled and paused, waiting for me to ask how.)

Me: Really, how? (I took the bait.)

Jonah: Well, you know how I got the iTunes gift card for my birthday for $10? I can use that for half.

Me: That's awesome, but how are you going to pay for the other $10?

Jonah: Well, I figured that you could pay for it. I mean, can you imagine both of us playing the game together? Spending quality time? Playing with the Steelers? Bonding? I would say that was worth ten bucks, wouldn't you, Daddy? (As he finished the sentence he looked up at me with big eyes and smiled, showing his dimples.)

Me: I would say so, bud. Thanks for thinking of me.

Jonah: No problem, Daddy. I just want to make sure you get quality time with me.

Me: Silent smile.

Now, I know that my son has watched me for many years

and has consciously and subconsciously picked up on some of my methods of communication, but I was tickled with this interaction.

- He put thought in to what he wanted.
- He mentally reviewed the objections that would come and how he would overcome them.
- He thought about when the best time and place would be to make his request so that he could maximize the chance of obtaining his desired outcome.
- He understood that I was the decision-maker here, but also was aware of who influenced my decisions: in this case, his mom.
- He reminded me of something we had already experienced (seeing the commercial), added perceived value to the item (graphics and enhanced rosters), then planted an emotional tie to my team (the Steelers).
- He had a response planned to offset my cost of purchase (the iTunes card) and then outlined a win for me that would justify my investment in the game (spending quality time with him).
- He used his physicality (smile and big eyes) when he asked for the game.
- All in all, he took me through a well planned and executed proposal and close.

As you think about my son's story, reflect on your own life and ask yourself if a similar situation has occurred that you can recall.

- Is there something that you asked your spouse to do and when you asked you altered your voice or body language

to seem sweet?
- Was there ever a time when you needed to ask your boss or staff for something and brought them a treat to ensure a yes?
- Can you recall a meeting where you wanted to get your point across, but first you offered a compliment or recognized someone's effort prior to offering your opinion?

Some would say that in each of these situations, you manipulated people to get your desired outcome. The word "manipulate" typically has a negative connotation as it suggests that you are influencing or taking control in an unfair or unscrupulous manner. I would respond that it isn't manipulation in this negative sense if it's for the good of everyone involved. You didn't manipulate, you enabled a mutually beneficial outcome—just like my son Jonah did. He got what he wanted, and he created a value for me as well. Win-win.

As an experiment, take notice as you go through your day or week to recognize when you act in a similar manner. Also, take notice of others doing the same thing, both in interactions with you and with others. Evaluate if all parties benefit from the exchange. I think you will see that people are engaged in "sales processes" all day, every day. People are using their communication skills to get what they want. If they do this with good intentions and offer value to themselves and others, then there is nothing wrong with this. If they are doing this with only their own interest in mind, then the manipulation of the interaction leads to a win-loss and is a recipe for disaster.

We will touch more on this subject in the pages to come. For the purposes of our time together here, I propose that all people who communicate (which is everyone on the planet), are involved in some sort of sales process—and therefore, everyone is in sales!

takeaways & key ideas

1. Everyone is in sales.
2. Sellers express a desire or belief that they want the buyer to accept.
3. Every customer "touch point" is a sales call.
4. We create situations every day in order to gain a desired outcome.
5. Ideal sales interactions are "win-win" for all involved.

considerations

1. In your selling environment, where are the additional customer touch points that can affect your sales outcome?
2. Can you recall a time when one of these "touch points" affected your overall sales outcome, either positively or negatively?
3. In your personal life, what types of "sales pitches" are you involved in daily?

4. When was the last time this happened? Who was involved? Who was the seller and who was the purchaser?

3

INTERNAL AND EXTERNAL SELLING

Many years ago, I was introduced to a concept that changed the way I do business. This concept was quite obvious but had been something that I was not consciously practicing daily. Once I embraced this concept, I not only increased my productivity and realized more success, but I also created a friendlier, peaceful, and more enjoyable environment in which to work. The concept is internal selling.

To understand this concept, let's first define terms. External selling is what you would typically perceive selling to be: selling to your customer base and the market that uses your product or service. Anyone who purchases your offering or any end user would also be included in this category. There is really nothing too complex about this.

Now let's define internal selling. This we define as selling your cause or desire to anyone within your organization who can help you achieve it. This includes anyone on your team who can help your goal or project, such as the marketing and leadership groups, the implementation and service staffs, administrative and clerical processing teams, and even other salespeople. Internal selling is essentially rallying the troops to get everyone on the same page with the same goal in mind. It is the concept of each person doing all that they can to help you achieve your goals. Once again, this can happen in a professional or personal environment, but let me start with an example of how this worked for me in a corporate setting.

When I started with Micros Systems, Inc., in 2006, I was surprised at how personal and intimate each sales transaction was to my team. This was new to me, as in my time with my previous company (AT&T), I sold products and services, and then handed over the sales orders to another department that would then finish off the process from there. I did not have to submit sales order paperwork for fulfillment. I did not have to contact engineering or customer service or a post sales team. I basically sold the products and then moved on to the next opportunity. This was the intentionally-designed sales process in a company with 40,000 employees.

At Micros, I worked in an environment where there were 100 people in one district office who supported a local territory. This office included sales, management, customer service, implementation, administration, and support teams, including an enhanced help desk. This meant that anything that I sold, and anything that I promised or implied in a pre-sales environment, was delivered by our local team. Furthermore, once I sold a deal, people in the same building would help me process the order and make sure that the paperwork was as it should be. They would also order equipment, program software, install the solution, and then introduce a support relationship for the years to come. This also meant that if anything went wrong with any part of the pre- or post-sales process, it would affect everybody in the office. As you can imagine, this put added pressure on the sales team to make sure that every sale was as clean as possible. If you had a messy sale or sold something "stinky," then everyone would smell it!

Now that I understood the environment of the Micros team, it was time to schedule one-on-one meetings with each of the department heads so that I could gain further clarity on the specifics of the process as well as identify the roles and responsibilities of my team. I saw this as an incredible opportunity to learn about the current process and begin to form relationships with each of my team members. It was during these initial meetings that I paved the path for future success by listening carefully and taking extensive notes. I made sure to start each meeting with an introduction that included some background on myself and how I ended up at Micros. But most important, after the pleasantries, I began the heart of the meeting with one important question: "What can I do, as a salesperson, to make your job easier, more effective, and more fun?"

As you can imagine, most people were taken aback when I posed this question, as they did not typically get asked this by new team members. Immediately, they let their guards down and the energy of the conversation shifted. As they would share with me, I took notes on everything. I recorded the challenges that they told me they faced daily, and how those challenges came to exist. I heard about the roadblocks, bottlenecks in processes, and all other pertinent information which inhibited success. I was an active listener as they described to me mistakes that others in my position had made. It was obvious that they were in the best position to help me have success. I recognized that they were instrumental in my future achievements, and I wanted to capitalize on their wealth of information. Most importantly, I realized that I had the ability to add to their success by being successful at what I did.

Additionally, I recorded personal information on each of them which I could use down the road. I would ask things such as the date of their birthday. Did they have children, and if so what were their ages? What sports team did they like? Did they have a favorite type of wine? Did they always stop for coffee in the morning? Did they go to the movies? Did they eat a certain type of candy? I took notice of some of their habits. I recorded this information in my phone contact list so that I could look them up and be reminded of it at any time.

As I worked with them over the years to come, I rewarded them at different times with little surprises that I knew they would enjoy. It was a thoughtful way to say "thank you" for helping me with a particular task or project. It was sometimes as simple as a Starbucks gift card or a chocolate bar. Often it could be a birthday or thank-you card after a project was completed. I used this practice regularly as I knew that these simple gestures conveyed my appreciation for a job well done—which at the end of the day would only add to the overall success of the sale.

I have known many successful executives and team leaders who check-in with their team on a regular basis. They may start their day with a walk around the office to say hello. This simple act of engagement offers a personal connection between co-workers. This can also happen via phone or email, although there is nothing better than a face-to-face interaction. Remember, your co-workers are people first, and employees second. Engage them personally and you will have a stronger relationship that will only help in a professional environment.

Internal selling can happen in your personal life as well. Simple acts of consideration can create an environment that is more pleasurable for you. For a moment, think about the last few days or weeks and recall any personal interactions that you may have had with your friends, family, or acquaintances. Were there any actions that you took to motivate someone else to do something for you? Was there something you did to enhance the possibility of getting a "yes" or confirmation that you were hoping for?

I propose that all of us have these moments as we go through life. This does not make us insincere . This is not merely an act of "buttering up" someone to get what we want, but rather maintaining an environment where constructive communication and openness to your idea can live.

Once again, internal selling as well as external selling need to exist together in an atmosphere where all parties receive value.

takeaways & key ideas

1. *Internal selling* is the process of selling your goals to anyone within your organization who can help you achieve it
2. Take notice of those who can help you and record what interests them so that you can personalize your appreciation later
3. The marriage of internal and external selling creates your best opportunity for success

considerations

1. Who in my organization can assist me with my project or goals?
2. Other than myself, who is most instrumental in my success?
3. How can I align with others in my organization to create a "team-win" environment?
4. Where does internal selling happen in your personal life?

part 2

NAVIGATING THE ENVIRONMENT

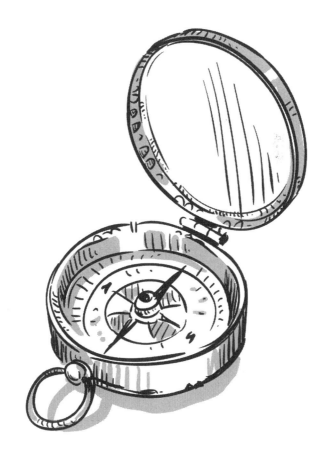

BECOME AN EXPERT

There is an adage mentioned in numerous texts which says that you must help yourself first so that you can then help others. This has application in many different arenas. If we spin it for our purposes here, I will state that before you can sell anything to anyone, you must first be an expert in whatever it is that you are selling. You must first help yourself by studying and researching the field, technology, service, or offering you will be representing. Only by doing so can you truly become an industry expert and be in a position that you can advise and guide your buying market.

On a broader scale, this happens in most professions. For example, doctors go to college and medical school for years prior to practicing medicine. Even after all this training they will continue to study, research medical topics, and engage in constant professional development in their field of expertise so they can stay up-to-date on new findings. Imagine if someone had the ability to become a doctor without studying. What if they could open a practice without credentials? How much confidence would you have in their ability to diagnose and treat you? Would you feel safe with their support and help? I'm sure not! We put our faith in doctors who are experts in their field, having demonstrated their openness to constant improvement.

Financial planners are another example of the necessity of professional expertise. You may decide to utilize a financial planner to help you manage your money and portfolio. You may have a combination of assets, retirement plans, and stocks which you need to ensure are secure and in a position to grow in value in the future. The stock market is a tricky thing with many variables that can offer great rewards or significant losses in the blink of an eye. International market activity, economic trends, politics, news events, and many other influences can cause great fluctuations in pricing from one second to the next. Your financial planner needs to have the background of how the market works from a global perspective. They need to know details about market leaders and trends, as well as key components that can affect your investments. They need to have expertise in the history of the markets as well as a concept of how general future projections will impact your overall financial plan.

> **Before you can sell anything to anyone, you must first be an expert in whatever it is that you are selling.**

Placing something as important as your financial future in the hands of another takes a great amount of trust and confidence in that person. This person needs to be an expert in their field with a proven track record and must have a wealth of knowledge so that they can make the best decisions to support your goals.

MY ROAD TO BECOMING AN EXPERT

When I was approached by Micros to come on board with them, I was not familiar with the inner workings of the hospitality industry or its technology. The solutions that Micros offered were hardware, software, and service offerings for hospitality environments which included restaurants, hotels, arenas, stadiums, universities, and any other institutional food service organizations. Although I was coming from another technology-based organization, and I knew how to sell, I was not familiar with the needs of either the industry or the individual segments and user groups listed above.

This was a bit different from other salespeople who had come aboard prior to my arrival, as most came from inside the hospitality industry. They understood the needs of the end user, had first-hand experience, and knew the buzzwords and industry jargon to communicate effectively with end users. I knew that if I were to succeed in this industry, I would need to study and learn everything I could about running such organizations.

I approached this systematically and focused on a few different key areas: market trends and economics, end user group similarities and differences, competitive offerings, and future development plans and projections. Let's take these one by one so that we can get an idea of the meaning of each and how to relate it back to what you are selling today.

Market Trends and Economics.

The first step that I took was researching the market that

I would be selling to. I looked to identify trends in market behavior. I asked questions such as these.

- How has the market changed in the last ten years?
- What were the key business metrics that judged market success?
- What were the top priorities of the market players? How had technology changed their business operations?
- How had their customers changed?
- How did they reach their customers?
- What was the stability of the current market?

Another key item to consider was the economic status of the buyer.

- Were they profitable?
- Were they more profitable today than in years past?
- What were they spending money on in their business?
- What were their margin levels on their offerings?
- What was constantly being developed inside of their business, and how did that affect their budgets?

By reviewing this information, I was able to grasp an overall understanding of the hospitality industry and learn about the hot topics which my customer base would have top of mind.

In your sales environment, you can approach the market in the same way. You may have variations to some of the questions above if you are selling not to a vendor or business but to end users instead. If this is the case, then you can simply apply the questions to that group. For example, when I first worked for AT&T, I ran a retail store where I would sell directly to the public. I reviewed the market in the same way but applied each of the questions directly to my customer.

- How has my customer base changed in the last ten years?
- What were their expectations of a vendor?
- What was important to them as they made their buying decision?
- What was their economic status?
- What were they spending their money on?

End User Group Similarities and Differences.

In the hospitality industry, there are many different customer types as well as user groups. As I did not have any experience in this industry prior to my time with Micros, I submerged myself in each of these groups to fully understand the industry from the inside out. I quickly identified trends of each segment and learned the importance of the elements of each. I noted the many differences between hotel operations and restaurant operations. Buying cycles, decision makers, budgets, functionality requirements, service expectations, integration availability, and more each painted extremely different characteristics of these groups. Conversely, there were many commonalities as well, which needed to be considered in any sales cycle. Additionally, there were also other segments in the industry which added to the overall market, including arenas, stadiums, universities, and other institutional feeders which had their own unique behavior and needs.

Through my research, I found that I could best understand each of these groups by attempting to walk a day in their shoes. If I was selling to a restaurant, I would ask to work a shift so that I could see what was happening on site during operations.

For a hotel, I would ask if I could shadow an employee for a period of time so that I could see firsthand what they were experiencing. If I could not be with them in person, then I would conduct phone interviews as necessary to capture all pertinent information. I would request time with all user groups so that I could fully understand and clearly identify any challenges for which I could provide solutions.

There are many types of sales to which the above example would not apply, although you still can uncover exactly who your user group is. Ask yourself these questions.

- Who is using this product or service?
- How are they using it?
- What solution can it provide for them?
- How large or small is this purchase of your solution to them?
- Do they have a budget for this service?
- Is this an impulse buy or is this a planned and budgeted asset purchase?
- How are other people or groups similar to the purchaser using the product or service?

By discovering the answers to these questions, you will identify the true needs of your customer base which in turn will match up to your products or solutions offered.

Competitive Offerings.
Another critical aspect of becoming an expert is knowing the competitive landscape in your industry. Competition is a good thing. It is actually a great thing! Competition keeps everyone honest and serves the customer at the end of the day by ensuring that pricing and purchasing terms are appropriate.

Knowing what your competition is doing and what they offer only adds to your overall expertise and adds credibility to you as an expert in your field.

Sellers today have the luxury of having all the data necessary for competitive analysis at their fingertips. By searching for any topic on the Internet, an abundance of information—from product specifications to user analysis and commentary—are available. This is an open source to become an expert on any topic. Furthermore, you can use the transactional experience itself to provide you additional information. Through the buying process, your customer has, no doubt, gathered his/her own information. They have also most likely already interacted with the competition. They have firsthand knowledge of the competitor's sales cycle, solution information, pricing, and approach, and you have an opportunity to get this information from them. This may or may not be shared openly with you, but there is no harm in asking for it.

For example, if you were selling a solution to a customer who did not have one in place thus far, you could ask them a series of questions.

- How has your experience been thus far in gathering your information?
- What surprises have you learned along the way?
- What solution elements have you been most impressed with?
- Is our product pricing on par with the others in the market?
- Is there anything negative about our solution that you have learned in your research that I can clarify for you?
- How does our service offering compare to the competitors?

Asking these questions can open lines of communication on the topic that are more valuable than any other research gathered. Although some buyers will hold their cards close to the chest and not want to share their findings, after the sale is completed, they may be more willing to reveal them. If they end up purchasing from you, they will most often share. If they do not purchase from you, then my suggestion is that you use the experience to learn by conducting a post-mortem on the lost opportunity. A few follow-up questions can offer insight to assist in future sales opportunities.

- I understand that you have made your final decision based upon your research, but can I ask for some feedback on our interaction during the process?
- What key elements were considered in your final purchasing decision?
- What were the top three reasons that made you choose the competitor's solution?
- Is there anything that I could have done differently to win your business?

While hearing the answers could sometimes be uncomfortable, they will provide invaluable insight. The main goal here is to analyze all offerings available to the customer and establish why someone would want to purchase your product over another's. What makes your offering better? Where do your strengths and weaknesses lie? Knowing this information is imperative as you navigate your market.

Future Development Plans and Projections.
As you think about the industry which you sell to, reflect on the trends and history that I discussed earlier in this chapter.

Think about how the trends and behavior have changed in the last year or two—or five, or even ten. Most industries have been affected by the technology advancements of the last ten years. With this in mind, ask yourself where the market is going.

- What changes are industry experts predicting?
- How will pricing change?
- What about the supply and demand of your product?
- Does the current offering have longevity, or will it be replaced by a newer, better solution in the coming years?
- How will the global economy affect your offering?
- What about market growth?
- What other competitive dynamics that may influence your success?

All of these items should be considered, as they will affect investment strategies today for your customer base. They are the winds that will either push you forward or push you off course, depending on how you prepare.

Over the last 10-15 years, many companies have been forced to deal with how the change in technology has altered the landscape of their business. Companies selling products and services from retail stores are now competing with online marketplaces. For example, the launch of Amazon Prime in 2005 introduced the concept of ordering nearly anything through your computer and having it delivered free to your doorstep within two days. They even added TV and movie streaming services some years later to sweeten their offering. Today, you can order goods and services through Amazon, and even have milk and eggs (and other groceries) delivered on demand. They have changed the culture of the consumer and the marketplace.

Those companies who have not adapted to this new surge in online sales may be suffering as they have lost a portion of their customer base. Companies with their finger on the pulse of the market have widened their online reach and perhaps decreased their retail brick and mortar footprint. Rest assured, you do not need to have a crystal ball to see in to the future. If you look for signs and follow industry commentary, you should be able to have a good idea as to where your industry is headed. Having this knowledge will add to your credibility and status as a trusted advisor.

Remember, your customer is coming to you to solve an issue for them. They will be more apt to purchase from someone who is an expert in their field. They will have the confidence in you to make them feel at ease about making the best decision. As an expert, you will be able to do these things for them.

- Inform them of the solution that you offer today.
- Tell them where the market has been and offer speculation on where it is going.
- Speak about industry topics and all credible players that have options for them.
- Identify their pain as you have spent time in their shoes and understand the challenges they face.

You will then use your knowledge and expertise to present a customized solution to fulfill their needs. Most likely at that point you will get the sale. But even if you don't, you will still get valuable information from them afterwards which will help you make the following sale.

takeaways & key ideas

1. Before you can sell anything to anyone, you must first be an expert in whatever it is that you are selling.
2. Study and research your industry to become an expert and trusted advisor.
3. Analyze market trends and economics, end user group similarities and differences, competitive offerings, and future development plans and projections. to gain a comprehensive understanding of your industry.
4. Subscribe to industry magazines, periodicals, RSS feeds, podcasts, forums, and blogs which can keep you on top of trends.

considerations

1. Do you consider yourself an industry expert today? If not, what can you do to ensure you become one? If so, what are you actively doing to stay on top of changing trends?
2. Where has your industry been? Where is it headed?

41

3. Who uses your products or services? How do they use them? How has this changed in the last 5-10 years? How do you think it will change in the next 5-10 years?
4. How are you positioned in the marketplace? How is your competition positioned?

IDENTIFY YOUR GOALS

One thing that is as important as spending the time and effort researching your field is the practice of setting goals so you know what you are working towards. Many of us understand the value of setting goals, but there are many reasons why we don't make this an everyday practice. To start, most have never been trained on how to set goals correctly. You most likely did not have a goal-setting class in grade school or high school. Your parents probably didn't teach you. And there were no textbooks on the power of goal setting. As a result, many of us do not set goals as we do not want to get teased or ridiculed when we set them. Others fear being rejected or simply fear failure. Whatever the reason may be, the practice of setting goals is not commonplace for most people today.

There is a benefit of setting goals that most people do not realize. A case study conducted in 2015 by Dr. Gail Matthews at the Dominican University in California found that the mere practice of setting goals enhances your ability to achieve them by nearly 43%. Furthermore, writing those goals down, creating action steps, sharing them with a friend or accountability partner, and adding progress report updates raises that achievement percentage up to 76%. That is a staggering revelation! Even the simple practice of creating goals and writing them down will make you twice as likely to achieve them.

The goals that you set need to have certain characteristics as well. The best way to remember these is to use the mnemonic S.M.A.R.T., created by George Doran, who first introduced these concepts in 1981 in the journal Management Review. This translates to Specific, Measurable, Agreed upon, Realistic, and Time-related. Let's explore each of these in more depth.

Specific.
The goals that you set need to have detail. Author and salesman Zig Ziglar said, "If you aim at nothing, you will hit it every time!" You need to make sure you have a target to aim at that is clear and detailed. The detail should be as granular as it can be. For example, if my goal is to have a breakout year in sales, that lacks both details and clarity. How do I define "breakout"? What type of sales am I referring to? In what market will I sell? To whom will I sell? The devil is in the details, which should be obvious to anyone who reads your goals.

Measurable.
This is the area where you will quantify your goals so that anyone reviewing them can have an accurate benchmark to determine if the goal is met or not. For example, if I refer to my previous statement of having a breakout year in sales, I need to quantify exactly what that means. How much revenue do I want to produce? How many units do I want to deliver? How much market share do I want to capture? How many new customers do I want to acquire? If I consider my breakout year to equate to $2 million dollars in revenue, then it is easy to determine if I complete that goal as I have a clear and mea-

surable target. If I reach $2 million, I have achieved my goal. If I miss that marker, I did not achieve my goal. This is pretty straightforward.

A side note on this is that you need to make sure that the measurable target is clear to all. If I say that my goal is to lose twenty pounds, there is no way for someone else to measure this unless they know my starting weight. If I say that my goal is to weigh 200 pounds, then it is possible for someone else to see if I do or not when I step on the scale. When creating a measureable goal, ensure that anyone can determine achievement without further explanation.

Agreed-Upon.
Goal "agreement" comes from clarifying who is responsible for the achievement of it. If you are setting a personal goal, then you alone are responsible for the outcome. If you are creating goals that involve others, then you will want to make sure to get everyone to agree upon the goals to which you are all committing. For example, in a sales environment, your goals should be in line with your quota or performance expectations. If this is a team goal, then your team should be able to commit to and agree upon the goal.

Realistic.
When setting a goal, you should make sure that it is possible given your knowledge, resources, and time. While it is one thing to set a goal that forces you to stretch yourself a little to attain it, use common sense. Some goals are simply impossible to achieve. For example, I once wanted to be a contestant on American Idol, but I was always older than the allowed age limit. If I set a goal to be a contestant on that show, it would

not have been realistic, as I did not meet the criteria in order to be considered for the show. If you are having issue with this or it becomes an area of confusion, ask yourself if the limitation or factor which prevents you from achieving this goal is true or not. Is this a universal truth or something that you may have made up to get out of doing it?

When I started at Micros, the district office that I was a part of never had a salesperson realize more than $1 million in sales in a single year. I set a goal to surpass $2 million in sales and win the Chairman's Award for the highest sales achievement in the company. Since it had never done it before, some said it was not realistic or possible. But just because no one has done it before does not mean that you cannot do it now. I set my goal, applied myself, produced more than $2 million, and captured the Chairman's Award the same year that I set the goal. Although it was difficult, it was not impossible. It became my reality.

Time-Based.
When setting goals, you will want to give yourself deadlines to achieve them. You should make these as specific as possible as well. If I say that I want to weigh 200 pounds next year, then when specifically, would that be: January or December? What day and time do I want to hold myself to? My weight goal should state that I want to weigh 200 pounds or less by December 1, 2019, at 12 p.m. PST. This adds detail to my goal. If you noticed, I also added the "or less" to my goal. You can also add an "or more." If my goal is to have $2 million in sales or more by December 31, 2018, at 5 p.m. PST, perhaps I will have $3 million in sales.

Another point to remember is not to put the goal too far out. Doing this can compromise your performance towards the goal. If I have a goal to be 200 pounds or less by December 1, 2020, at 12 p.m. PST, then perhaps I will not be concerned about a healthy diet until late in 2019. Once again, the time allowed for your goals to be achieved should be obvious to anyone who reads them. There should be no ambiguity, and it should be in a time frame that inspires you to work towards it today.

Goals can be, and should be, part of your everyday practice in every area of your life. I would recommend that you set goals in each of the following areas.

- Professional (work, career)
- Relationships (family, friends, romance)
- Health (fitness, exercise, diet)
- Financial (income, net worth)
- Recreation (fun time, vacations, hobbies)
- Personal (possessions, growth and development, education)
- Contribution (philanthropy, community, service)

By setting goals in each of these areas you are setting yourself up for success in every area of your life.

Examples of goal formulation
Good: I will lose fifty pounds by summer.
Better: I will weigh 200 pounds by December 1, 2017, at 12 p.m. PST.

Good: I will own a beach house.
Better: I will own a five-bedroom beach house in Redondo Beach, California, with an ocean view, pool, gym, and in-home

theater.

Good: I will write a sales book.

Better: I will write a New York Times best-selling book that details my most important and successful sales strategies by Jan 31, 2019.

The Breakthrough Goal

Another type of goal that has incredible impact is the stretch or breakthrough goal. This is the kind of goal that once achieved would catapult you to a new level of accomplishment or success. For example, I might say that I have a goal to write a best-selling book, convert China to a buying market, find my soulmate and get married, buy a five-bedroom house, or conduct a keynote speech at the Staples Center. This breakthrough goal may seem like it is too far out of reach and thus unrealistic. But this is where you could take a leap of faith and push yourself out of your comfort zone to achieve it. Author and motivational speaker Jim Rohn said, "You want to set a goal that is big enough that in the process of achieving it you become somone worth becoming."

Process Goals

As you set your goals, remember that all goals are not the same size. This is okay and normal. A process goal is a smaller goal that assists in the accomplishment of a larger one. These

> ❝ *You want to set a goal that is big enough that in the process of achieving it you become someone worth becoming. - Jim Rohn*

process goals can either be the step-by-step actions you take to achieve your ultimate goal or the benchmarks you use to recognize success. For example, when my goal was to reach $2 million in sales, I had process goals to reach $167,000 each month so that I could stay on track for reaching my larger goal. For additional goal setting worksheets, visit my website at www.captureyourpower.com/resources.

The Rule of 5

Success coach, author, and speaker Jack Canfield explains a concept in his book The Success Principles which he refers to as "The Rule of 5." He recalls the advice he received from Ron Scolastico, a wonderful teacher, who told Jack that, "If you would go every day to a very large tree and take five swings at it with a very sharp ax, eventually, no matter how large the tree, it would have to come down."

This principle suggests that regardless of the magnitude of your goal, if you create and execute five steps daily that will get you closer to that goal, then sooner or later you will accomplish it. My recommendation is to write down five things daily that you can do to advance you closer to achieving your goal. Share these with a friend or partner and check in regularly with them for accountability.

The Power of Visualization

Once you have created goals that are clear, specific, and measurable, the next step is to visualize yourself achieving those goals. Did you know that when you visualize, you activate your brains Reticular Activating System (RAS) that manages your neural pathways and stimulates your consciousness? By doing this, you program your brain to look for existing resources around you which can help you achieve your goals. You also program your brain to be aware of any new resources that come in to your life that can be used to make your visualizations come true. Once you trigger the RAS with your visualization, you create structural tension (the difference between your desired state and the actual state) that then shifts your perception. Through this process, you force your brain to filter out all that isn't needed and solely concentrate on what will assist in making this visualization a reality.

Additionally, your brain does not realize the difference between a visualization and reality. To exercise my point, take a moment after reading this to close your eyes and visualize the following scene.

You are at an amusement park and step up to the front of the line at the fastest roller coaster at the park. You look down and notice the tips of your shoes just behind the yellow line painted on the floor with the words "Do Not Pass" in bold lettering. To your left, you can hear the clinks of the roller coaster cars slowly climb the hill to the tallest peak of the ride. To your right, you can hear the distant screams of the riders on the roller coaster and catch a glimpse of the cars circling the loop at the far end of the attraction. You hear voices behind you and can feel a combination of nervous energy and excitement brewing in the air. Suddenly, you are being escorted by the attendant to your seat in the front car of the coaster. As you sit down on the hard, sturdy seat, the security bar lowers to lock your legs in place. You look up to see the somewhat sinister smile of the attendant as he says, "Have a nice ride," while your car exits the station. As you begin to climb the hill to the tallest peak of the ride, the loudness of the clinks of the car are only offset by the beauty of the view of the entire park from your vantage point. As you reach the top, the clinks stop, and everything pauses as you momentarily are still… only moments later realizing that you are starting your descent down the other side of the hill, gaining speed as you go. The speed of the car combined with the screams behind you catch your breath, and all you can do is hold on for dear life …

Did you feel anything in your body change as you committed to this exercise? Did you feel as if you were on the roller coaster and get butterflies? Was there any physical reaction to your visualization process? Did you feel any nervousness, anxiety, or excitement? This is common. When you imagined the ride, your brain thought that you were on that roller coaster and the same physical effects occurred as you had actually been there.

So how do you use this in your sales environment? Through visualization, you can create an environment where you are already living the result of your goals before you actually achieve them. You can feel these results, see them, taste them, smell them, and hear them. Your goal can become real in your mind before it manifests in reality. This is a "practice run" of sorts so that you can investigate and accept all elements of the outcome of the goal.

When I set my goal to produce $2 million in sales and capture the Chairman's Award, I visualized myself getting my bonus check for my efforts and feeling pride as I received accolades and congratulations from my peers. I imagined myself on stage being handed the award from the president of the company. I envisioned what I was wearing, seeing, hearing, smelling, and most importantly, feeling. I imagined what impact this achievement would have on my personal finances. At that time, I was saving for my first home and knew that it would help me purchase it. I envisioned where I would live and the pride I would feel walking in to a home that I owned. All of these visions were connected to this one goal. The further detail and clarity that I gave it made it more real and kept it at the top of my mind every day that I went to work. The vision produced the reality.

Setting goals is an integral part of success. Making these goals clear, specific, and measureable is a requirement. Writing these goals down and sharing them with a friend will make you even more successful. Finally, periodically offering progress reports or updates to your friend will make you accountable for your goal achievement.

Following this goal-setting practice is part of every successful person's success, both personally and professionally. If you are not setting goals today, start. Set small ones at first if you need to but do it. Congratulate yourself when you achieve them. Celebrate and reward yourself for your hard work. As you continue this process and make this a habit, your goals will grow, as will your success. This I promise you!

takeaways & key ideas

1. Setting goals is an integral part of anyone's success.
2. Simply writing down your goals doubles your chance of obtaining them.
3. Use the SMART method of goal setting and share them with a partner for accountability.
4. Set a breakthrough goal.
5. Use The Rule of 5 daily.
6. Reinforce your goals with visualizations.

considerations

1. What goals have you defined in each of the areas of your life? (professional, relationships, health, financial, recreation, personal, contribution)
2. With whom will you share your goals with and report your progress?
3. What is your breakthrough goal?
4. How can you use the Rule of 5 and process goals to advance you towards goal achievement?

SALES MARKET STRATEGY

At this point you have researched your field, captured information, and learned behaviors that will make you an industry expert. You have also set goals so that you know what you are working towards. You understand that your level of expertise will grow, and your goals will shift along your journey. You are excited and flexible and know that you are on your way to sales prosperity. The next item on your plate is to create a market strategy that will give you the best chance of success. In your current sales position, you may have territories, channels, verticals, or sub-segments of customers that populate your market. Regardless of the make-up, the areas and strategies that we will discuss next can apply to many different industries, fields, and selling environments.

Let's start with an overview of your market approach. Sales success is a numbers game. The more opportunities you have, the more likely you will be to close more deals. The more sales you close, the more money you make. Simple, right? So how do you close the most deals? You do this by picking apart your sales market, identifying your varying opportunities, and working each opportunity with a well-thought-out game plan.

Inside your market, you will have some sales that come very easily. These are opportunities referred to as your "warm or qualified leads." These people are repeat buyers or fans who are already interested and ready to purchase. These are typically opportunities that come to you, rather than you going out and uncovering them. Although these leads may show up easily, they still require being taken through the sales cycle to ensure that customers fully understand your offering and the value that it provides them.

> " *Sales success comes from picking apart your market, identifying your opportunities, and working each opportunity with a well thought out game plan.*

The opposite of a warm lead is a cold one. They represent everyone else who is a possible customer. Cold calling is the process where you are engaging with a new potential customer without knowing if there is any interest at all. Although cold calling is a necessary part of a sales career, this varies depending on what your product or service is. For example, if you have a position in sales at a storefront of any kind, whether this is a car dealership or a mobile phone retail store, you have potential customers that physically walk in to your establishment. These are warm leads. If you are selling credit card services to businesses via phone across the United States, then you are making calls to people who are on your list, but you have no idea if they are interested in your service or offering. These are cold calls.

In any type of sales, there are always ways to create more opportunities. If the outcome is to uncover all opportunities that are possible, you will need to create a strategic plan on how to work your area, and then work that plan daily. As noted above, allocating time on warm leads will produce the best results, as your conversion rate is highest with this group. Additionally, you will need to dedicate time to cold calling as well as this produces some results, even if fewer. Finally, identifying opportunities where you can gain multiple sales from one single effort is critical. This may take longer and be more complicated, but it will push your production and revenue over the top when they finally come to fruition. These opportunities we refer to as whales. Through a combination of these elements, you are approaching your market from different angles and will create the best chance for success.

Years ago, I had the opportunity to work with a bright young sales rep named Charles. I coached and mentored Charles as he began a new position where his responsibilities were to sell payroll and merchant services for a large organization. Charles was a great student, hungry for success and ready to work hard, which made him a joy to spend time with! When he started with his company, he was assigned a territory in greater Los Angeles County, and his primary focus was retail and food service businesses. This territory was a large area which included many cities, and initially he wondered how he would cover it all. I assured him that we could create a strategic plan that, if executed, would produce results greater than he imagined.

First, we started with what we knew. We knew that he was going to target retail and food service businesses and organizations in a specific geographic area. We knew that they all had the same Standard Industrial Classification (SIC) code, which is the system in the United States for classifying industries by a four-digit code. We accessed a list of zip codes for the cities that were in his area from the US Postal Service website. We then searched the Internet for a website which enabled us to pull a list of standard industry codes (SIC) that were organized by zip code, which then we plugged in to a working map on his computer. This showed us all of his opportunities and where they were in his territory. We then created zones on this map and numbered them 1 to 10. We knew that when he began he would attack zone 1, knocking door to door, until he had covered that area completely. He would then work his way through all zones and when complete, cycle through them again starting with the first. This would ensure that he covered all leads in the process. This also gave him an intimate perspective of this industry from those on the ground floor and created a knowledge base which he could not have obtained any other way.

Another component of being fruitful in his territory was to identify all possible large sales opportunities. In the retail and hospitality field, this would apply to any large chains or organizations that had multiple outlets. Of course, we knew a few of these names already as we lived in the area and frequented many of these chains. But we also referred to the SIC reports as they provided a company profile for each listing which showed annual revenue and the employee base size. There are many websites that can provide this information, although the one that we used most often was Hoovers (www.Hoovers.com).

As he set out each day to work different areas in his territory, he would have these larger accounts in the back of his mind so that if he ran across them he could learn, take notes, ask questions of staff, take notice of on-site operations, and meet local management. This would come in handy if, and when, he found himself in a sales opportunity later as it would show that he knew their business well.

He also submerged himself in industry events that would provide opportunities to meet industry experts. These events included trade shows, networking mixers, and special events. I suggested that he join several groups that were connected to this industry, such as the local chamber of commerce, Rotary Club, and professional organizations in an effort to gain exposure and create relationships with the local business owners and leaders.

Now, as a reminder, there is no silver bullet in sales. Some enter this field in the hopes of quick success, but there is no getting around hard work. In his first year or two, he knocked on doors daily and worked diligently to create results in his market. He created relationships with on-site managers and staff. He met owners and leaders at local industry events as well. He eventually became known as "the guy" that people needed to talk to when they purchased payroll and merchant services. He planted seeds daily. Some germinated quickly, and others took years to harvest. By approaching his territory from different angles, he created opportunity after opportunity. He experienced such a level of success that every prior sales record was shattered from his efforts.

High-level success comes from applying creative and methodical thinking to your sales environment. How can you pick apart your market opportunities to create the best chances of success? How can you approach your prospects in new and different ways? How can you create a plan to have the highest probability of success, quota achievement, or market penetration? What can you do differently than your competitor that will work for you? By constantly asking yourself these questions you will push yourself in to new levels of achievement, and ultimately become more successful.

takeaways & key ideas

1. Your sales success will come from a combination of different market segments and sources, including small and large opportunities.
2. Plan your work, and then work your plan.
3. Every market can be broken down into smaller pieces to be more approachable.
4. There is no silver bullet; you must do the work.

considerations

1. What are the largest opportunities in your market?
2. How can you approach your specific market from different angles?
3. What tools, resources, and/or people can help you penetrate your market most effectively?
4. What actions can you take daily which will have the greatest impact on your market?

THE SALES PROCESS

Once you have ascertained the market strategy and have a plan to attack your territory, you will work new opportunities on a regular basis. The next step is to introduce a unique sales process that you will apply to each of these opportunities so that you can move them towards a final solution, and ultimately a close. This process can be used in any and every sales environment and should become so ingrained in you that you can implement it without a second thought. Remember, sales is a numbers game. Each opportunity is your chance to take a swing at your territory and quota. Each sale won will leave an indentation on your overall required deliverables. By utilizing a sales process, you will always know exactly where you are and what the next step will be to move towards a close or outcome. It takes the guess work out of your action plan.

Before I explain the steps of the sales process, we will need to agree that one specific requirement is a thorough understanding of your offering and the value that it brings to your potential customers. (See Chapter 4, "Becoming an Expert.") By having this comprehensive insight, you will be able to match the features or benefits of your offering to a specific need of the customer. This direct correlation will help to facilitate a more efficient journey through the sales process and increase your chances of a successful close. As we define the specific steps of this sales process, we will use the mnemonic INDENT so that it is easier to remember.

- Identify prospects
- Needs analysis
- Demonstrate / Present
- Empathize and handle objections
- Negotiate
- Take order / close

This can also be represented in its cyclical process seen in the following graph.

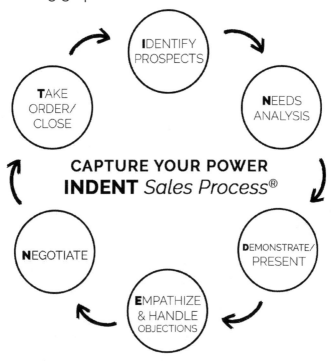

Identify prospects.

Before you can go out and sell anything, you need to iden-tify who are the best and most suitable customers who can purchase your product, service, or solution.

If you are in a retail environment, then your prospects may be anyone who walks through your door. If you have a terri-tory, then you would need to canvas your area and contact potential prospects in an effort to convert them to qualified leads. These potential prospects can be reached through direct door-to-door interaction, phone campaigns, website contact lists, direct mailings, marketing efforts, social media campaigns, trade shows and conventions, or other events where you have direct access to interested parties. As mentioned in the last chapter, you will have various types of prospects; small, large, independent, corporate, and non-conventional. Your goal is to qualify that they are worthy of going to the next round of the sales process. Ask yourself the following questions.

- Are they ready to buy?
- Do they have a budget?
- Is this a good fit?
- Does this solve a business need for them?
- Can they make the decision to purchase? If not, who can?
- How much is it costing them to not purchase your solution?

Most of these are questions that can be answered quickly at the beginning of your interaction with the prospect. The other questions are items that can be logged initially and uncovered down the road through your process. If you determine them to be a qualified prospect, then the next and most important question to ask is this: "When would be a good time to meet for a discovery session so that I can learn more about your needs?"

Needs Analysis.

Once you have identified your qualified lead or prospect, the next step is to identify the needs of that customer. Ultimately, you will match the needs that you uncover with the features of your product or solution and convey the value or benefit that is created from the marriage of those two. At times, the needs of the customer may seem very straightforward. Other times, you may engage with a prospect who feels that they need to purchase something, but they are not sure why, and they require assistance with getting clarity on the topic. Either way, your task is to bring to light the problem or issue that they are attempting to solve.

The best and most efficient way to uncover the true needs of the customer is to spend time with them and ask questions. Regardless of your sales environment, there are common questions that can initiate the opportunity for further dialogue on the subject. Start with the most obvious questions based around who, what, when, why, and how.

- Who needs this product, service, or solution?
- What exactly are they hoping to get from it?
- When do they need it?
- Why do they need it in this time frame?
- Why do they need this solution for their business or personal life?
- How is having this solution going to help them?

Although these seem like very simple questions, they are a

very effective way to start the conversation. The answers that you receive will provide the backstory of the opportunity and enable you to gain further insight to the customer's motivation for seeking out a solution. Imagine that you are a painter with a blank canvas. The questions that you ask and answers you receive will help create the image. The image that you create will depict the current situation without your solution as well as the desired outcome after they have your solution in place.

In my time spent with Micros, I worked with thousands of prospects both large and small. Although there were similarities in each opportunity, all had their own unique set of needs. Many years ago, I worked with a small but prestigious restaurant in Santa Monica, California. This restaurant had been operating for over forty years when I was introduced to them through a mutual associate. I was familiar with this restaurant and its reputation in the area and started to "diagnose" their problems before I had even met with them. When I met with the owner (Mike), I began to ask questions and listen to his story. I asked him to tell me why he was in search of a solution for this business.

As he spoke, I learned about the operations of his business and his need to update his technology. He told me about the manual systems he had in place and how they had worked well for over forty years. He validated many of the things that I had "pre-diagnosed" about his business, and shared backstory on the business' inception and journey through the years. See, over time, Mike found that he was spending more and more time at the restaurant as his business grew. His financials were difficult to manage, and his payroll was out of control. As I continued to dig and move beyond the surface, I learned that there were no operational checks and balances in place. Additionally, he mentioned that he would work late nights and weekends to balance the books.

As we picked apart each of these items, he explained to me the process of the late night and weekend balancing. The following is a paraphrase from memory of our general conversation.

Mike: At the end of each week, I pull all of the register tapes from both registers from each night along with the sales tickets for each transaction. I pull three tables together and lay each day's transaction receipts out on the table with the corresponding tickets. I then start with Monday's transactions and validate all totals by checking the math on each ticket to ensure that everything was accounted for correctly. Once validated, I log each one into my accounting journal for the day. I do this for each day of the week and then create a spreadsheet for the week that shows the totals. Next, I collect all time cards for each of the employees for the week and spread them out on the tables. There are 15 employees who use the time clock, so each have their own time card with multiple time punches on their card. I match these time punches up to the schedule to ensure that everyone has been on time and then identify any overtime that has occurred. I log this information in to our labor journal for the week and then staple the time cards to the schedule. I collect all of the receipts, register tapes, time cards, and associated paperwork for the week and put it in a folder and file it our cabinet in the closet.

Me: Wow! That sounds like a pretty thorough routine. What happens if there is a discrepancy on a time card?

Mike: If there is a discrepancy, then I investigate it the following day, but it takes more time.

Me: What happens if a ticket is lost or if the register tape doesn't match the handwritten receipt?

Mike: If there is a lost ticket, it can take a while to investigate. Lost tickets can be just a careless error by the staff or can be a sign of something more serious, such as employee theft. If register tapes don't match, then we need to pull out all of the paperwork and dig through everything again to search for the answers. This has happened before and has caused us to be here all night at times.

Me: All night? Wow, how long would the whole process take if you had no issues at all?

Mike: If we had no issues, then we could get it done in about eight hours.

Me: Eight hours? That's a commitment! And how long did the process take the last time you had an issue?

Mike: The last time this happened, we were here all weekend working on it. We worked on it all Friday night after closing and did not resolve it until early Monday morning. I would say that we spent about twenty hours trying to figure it all out. It was not the best way to spend our anniversary!

Me: Was it the restaurant's anniversary?

Mike: No, my wedding anniversary.

Me: Did you have to put your anniversary plans on hold until you figured this out?

Mike: No, my bookkeeper is my wife.

Me: Wait, so every week when you reconcile your financials and payroll, you and your wife are here doing it together?

Mike: Yes. The business was not always this busy, but as business increased, so did my time at the restaurant. My wife offered to help with the books so that I could finish earlier, and we could have our weekends together. Over time, we found ourselves spending every weekend at the restaurant and not having any other quality time.

Me: So, getting a new solution is not only so that you can add efficiencies to your business, but also so that you can capture some time back to spend with your wife.

Mike: Absolutely! I have a long list of things to catch up on!

As you can imagine, I was blown away by this conversation. I spent nearly two hours with Mike before this information was delivered. I initially thought that I had it all figured out. I thought I knew what his issues and motivation would be for purchasing a new solution. It was only through the process of asking multiple questions and digging deeper and deeper that I discovered the issue that he truly wanted to solve. Of course, I learned that he had valid business needs for adding a new solution to his operation. There was no doubt that the new technology would benefit him in the recording and tracking of his financials and payroll. There were many benefits that his business would receive, both for his operations staff and management. What came as a surprise is that the most important issue to him was the amount of time that was required to finish the daily and weekly tasks. I don't believe that this was obvious to him when we began our conversation, but as we continued to speak, I could see that he had an epiphany. If he implemented a new solution, he would be able to recapture his lost weekends with his wife. This was his win.

In addition to the obvious needs of a business owner or main purchaser, it is important to consider any other parties involved with or affected by the solution that you are presenting. This could be user groups, partners, spouses, or others associated with the business. For example, with the restaurant mentioned above, I identified that the general manager, kitchen manager, and Mike's wife would all use the solution in some capacity. It was important for me to spend time with each of them to assess their needs and gain an understanding of how they would use the new system.

Another sales experience that comes to mind is when I sold to a hotel property. During this interaction, I met with the hotel's owners, general manager, food and beverage managers, CFO and accounting staff, front desk manager, catering and special events departments, and the IT staff. Each of these groups had their own specific needs involved with a new technology solution at their property, and each had the ability to influence the buying decision in their own way. By spending time with each department and identifying their needs, I built the value of the solution by addressing their needs specifically. Additionally, it was easier for the CEO and decision makers to make the final decision, as all of the departments endorsed the solution. Looking back on the interaction with Mike, I am reminded that there is always more information to grasp. Ask questions; then listen. There is an adage that says, "You have one mouth and two ears, so listen twice as much as you speak." This is very true in a sales environment. If you ask open-ended questions, enable your prospect to speak, and listen attentively, your answers will come. The needs of the prospect will present themselves.

Demonstrate/Present.
The next step in the sales process is the product, service, or solution demonstration or presentation. During this step, you will collect the information that you gathered from your needs analysis and tie each one of the benefits or features of your

solution back to a specific need. Although the demonstration or presentation can be a formal or informal process, dependent on the sales environment and opportunity, there are always preparation items to check on and questions to ask prior to the event. These items may include the following.

- If you have the need to use or display equipment, is there somewhere for you to set this up?
- What presentation tools will you be using? Will there be a PowerPoint presentation utilized? Will you use a projector? Is there a screen or empty wall available to project upon? Is the lighting in the room sufficient for showing a PowerPoint? Do you have a hand-held slide clicker or advancement tool? Do you need a laser pointer?
- Is there sufficient power in the room? Do you need extension cords or surge protectors?
- Where will you be conducting the presentation? If in a conference or board room, are there a sufficient number of chairs?
- Do you need Internet access for the presentation? Is there a hard-wired connection or Wi-Fi available in the presentation room?
- Have you confirmed a list of attendees? Do you know their title and correct spelling of their name? Have you met with them or spoken to each attendee or someone in their department?
- Will you have anyone from your own team at the meeting to support you? Perhaps a technical expert or manager? What will each person's role be in that meeting?
- Have you created an agenda for the meeting that you can print and distribute to each meeting attendee?
- Have you confirmed the amount of time that you will need

to present your solution?
- What time of day will you be meeting? Do you need to bring in coffee, snacks, or lunch?
- Do you have business cards to leave with each attendee?
- Do you have leave-behind material, marketing brochures, or solution information to give to your contacts?
- Have you considered if a joint meal after the meeting with your contacts would be appropriate?

Conducting a successful demo or presentation can be an arduous task in and of itself. There can be many variables that easily throw you off task, so you should always have an agenda that has been agreed upon by yourself and the customer. This agenda should include the information that you want to deliver and should be of importance to the customer. The way to ensure this is to connect each solution element back to solving a customer's need. An easy way to check to this is to ask yourself why the customer cares about this for each topic presented. If the answer is "I don't know" or "I'm not sure," then you have some additional discovery to do on that topic. The last thing you want is to find yourself in a presentation telling the customer about something that they do not find valuable or do not care about. This will not end well. With diligent discovery of their needs you should be able to effectively match the solution benefits with the customer needs and ensure that the value of what you are selling is clear.

Another key ingredient of a successful demonstration or presentation is the pacing, or timing of your delivery. Remember, you want to show the customer that you are an expert in your field by speaking confidently about the solution you are presenting. With that being said, do not expect that the customer knows or can digest all of the knowledge that you are presenting. It is important to check in with the customer throughout the meeting. An easy way to do this is to stop after each topic or section of your presentation and simply ask them if it is clear and offer to address any questions they may have at that point. Then ask them if it is okay to move on to the next topic.

While conducting your presentation, be aware of your environment and audience. You will learn a lot through their feedback and body language. Remember, the agenda is a guide to show you where you are going but can be changed or modified as necessary. If you sense that a topic needs further discussion, then you can pause and suggest that you spend a few more minutes to review. There will be times where you are delivering your solution elements and something will seem off or uncomfortable in the meeting setting. There may be puzzled facial expressions, people shifting uncomfortably in their chairs, or murmuring among themselves. It is possible that a topic discussed has raised the customer's awareness of a separate issue that may or may not have been discussed. Again, it is okay to pause and dig in to this to ensure that all, important topics have a chance to be discussed.

In some sales settings, you may have audience members in attendance with whom you have not had a chance to spend time and review their specific needs or concerns. This may be someone who was not a part of the discovery process but was invited to the presentation to review the proposed solution. This person could be a business partner, a board member, a spouse, or someone in a supportive role in a relevant department. Regardless, it is important to canvass all attendees prior to starting the presentation to redefine their needs and goals. This can be done in a few different ways depending on the setting and circumstances of the meeting. You can simply ask them to summarize what they are hoping to get from the meeting. Or ask them to confirm what their main goals for a new solution are x, y, and z.

If you are in a larger setting with several attendees, then before you get started, go around the room so that each attendee can introduce themselves, give their title or department, and offer one or two things that they are hoping to learn or take away from today's presentation.

This will give you the chance to put faces to names and make notes of key areas of importance for each of your audience members. Additionally, this process will restate for the group the goals of the presentation.

Although we will always hope for a smooth and engaging presentation, there may be times where you get thrown a curveball. This may arise at any point from any audience member, and you must be ready to address it and handle each delicately and appropriately. There may be an attendee who wants another solution and makes it their mission to attend the meeting and refute your solution's value. They may want the competitor's solution as they prefer that one. They may have a grudge against you, your company, or your solution in general which you have no idea about. They may take the "sniper" approach and only speak up in the meeting to create conflict or offer negative input on the topic. In each case, you will need to react. You will need to make the choice whether to stop the presentation and address the item directly or suggest to table it and address it at a later time. In any event, staying calm, professional, and as transparent as possible is the best response. Remember, you are in control of your presentation and can facilitate it as you need to.

Preparing a script for the presentation is the best way to ensure that your delivery is clear and concise. A script should be created and used as a guide to identify and rehearse key terminology or convey specific points as intended for optimal consumption by your audience. Understandably, you cannot and would not want to script every word, but you can practice ahead of time the delivery of key selling points and ideas. It will be easier for you to remember these bullet points as you give more presentations and your experience grows.

Additionally, your script should include any items that may include live product functionality reviews if applicable. For example, if you were in digital media sales or social media marketing, you could script and practice the PowerPoint presentation of your offering as well as the transitions to a live website through your presentation. This process would ensure that the delivery was smooth, clear, and easy to follow for your prospect.

Another area of consideration in a demo and presentation is the technology used to aid you in the process. Technology should enable you to demonstrate your point but should not be a distraction in the process. There can be a very fine line between these two, and feedback and experience will be your guide regarding what and how much of anything to use. If you use a PowerPoint presentation, then there are some general rules that you should apply as well. Here are some PowerPoint guidelines as a reference.

- **Choose color schemes and slide designs carefully.** Make sure colors are warm and complementary. Maintain a theme and choose color schemes wisely to support your messaging. Review slides from a visual perspective and ensure that the text, font, and backgrounds are easy to see, interpret, and digest.
- **Coordinate headings, text, and font.** Make sure that fonts are consistent in size, placement, style and color. Utilize global settings to ensure and enforce consistency rules. Less is more. Utilize bullet points that state key words or phrases. Do not include full explanations on topics that you can speak to. Doing so will steal your thunder.
- **Do not read every word on the slide.** Please, please, please—do not read every word on the screen. We have all sat through meetings where someone is presenting something via PowerPoint and they read each word on the screen. This is painful and sometimes referred to as "Death by PowerPoint." Our audience naturally reads ahead and then waits for the presenter to catch up. This can cause distraction and lack of interest. Be advised—your audience can read. They are not stupid. To ensure that your PowerPoint serves as an aid and does not become a hindrance, only include key words or bullet points that you can elaborate on.
- **Minimize animations and images.** Again, there is a fine line between too much and too little. Start with small, selective choices and then grow from there. You will figure out what works and what does not throughout the process.
- **Make backup copies of the file.** Make a backup copy of the file on a flash drive which you carry with you. Also,

store a backup copy on Dropbox, Google Drive, or another cloud-based storage solution. With access to these backup copies, you will ensure that you have access to this critical information in the event that your laptop, equipment, or file fails or is corrupted or stolen.

- **Review, review, review.** Use your slide sorter to review the overall look, feel, and flow of the presentation. Go through transitions in your slides to establish smooth progressions. Be open to modify or change the order of your slides based upon feedback and experience.
- **Customize each presentation.** Make sure to customize the presentation for each customer or prospect. You can use core content that conveys your solution elements and message but try to personalize it as much as possible to your unique audience.

Your demonstration and presentation should be well-organized, well-planned, well-rehearsed, and well-executed. You should be flexible and ready for changes or modifications that may come up at any time. If you know your material and are well-versed with the presentation aids, then you can respond quickly and not have it throw you off course. Remember, the main goal of the demo and presentation is to get buy-in from the customer on the value of your solution. Once you receive their confirmation that they see the benefits of the solution and the opportunity to address their needs, then you can move them to the next phase of the sales process.

Empathize and Handle Objections.
There is an art to handling objections that can be perfected over time through experience. At the core of this are a few simple steps. These include restating the objection, empathiz-

ing, and repositioning. Let me provide a simple example and assume that you are purchasing a new computer.

Objection
Customer: If I purchase a new computer system I will have to learn how to use it and that will slow my work down.

Restate
Salesperson: So, to be clear, your primary concern with a new computer purchase is that the learning curve will be difficult, and your work will suffer, is this correct?

Customer: Yes, that is correct.

Empathize
Salesperson: I understand that learning a new computer program or system can be a challenging task and that you cannot afford for your work to suffer.

Reposition
Salesperson: Did you know that there are many different tools that are built in to the new system which aid with your learning curve? These include automated tutorials and support files to enable that you learn quickly. Also, there are user forums that can be accessed to post questions that are managed directly by our support staff.

Customer: No, I did not realize that.

Salesperson: Our main goal with providing a new computer system is to make the work you do more efficient. Once you complete minimal training, you should be able to work at a faster pace than ever before.

This simple engagement can be complimented by utilizing the "Felt/Found" positioning, as follows.

Customer: I know that the system is supposed to help, but I'm still concerned about the transition.

Salesperson: I understand your concern. You know I recently worked with another business owner in the area who **felt** the same way, and he **found** that after he purchased the new system he was working at a faster rate within one week.

The "Felt/Found" method is most effective when referencing someone recognized by the customer. For example, if I were selling a new solution to a restaurant, I might reference a neighboring restaurant that had already implemented the solution. Also, I would use personalized names as much as possible, as in, "Mike up the street felt this way as well, but he found that his productivity skyrocketed in the first week." This personalization would help paint a clearer picture for the customer.

Typically, there will be follow-up items that arise throughout the demonstration and presentation process. These could come up during or after the meeting as items of inquiry that need further clarity. With each of these items, it is important to log the objection and address it in depth with the concerned party. Do not be discouraged when objections come up. They are actually buying signals that give you the opportunity to offer further explanation on your solution. Again, your goal is to remove any roadblocks in the process. By knowing about them, you can address them and overcome these obstacles.

As you address each of these objections, practice the re-statement of the concern to ensure that there is agreement on exactly what the issue is, and schedule time to address these items with the appropriate person who expressed the issue. This may lead to additional visits with a decision maker and enable you to spend more time with the prospect. This also may lead you to uncover further new information. In a larger sales environment, you should expect that follow-up meetings with different user groups will be needed to ensure that you address each one's specific needs. In these situations, you can conduct a deeper dive of the solution elements that you may have not had the chance to do in the first meeting.

If you present a solution for an organization who has many different departments or a large board of directors, you may encounter different individuals who have influence on the final decision. In this situation, it is important to address each of their needs specifically. You can guide your efforts or team through the process of discovery sessions with all different department heads and their supporting staff. As the solution may have many complexities, you should expect that there will be objections and further clarity needed on numerous topics. During the solution presentation, as objections arise, be sure to log each one and schedule follow-up visits to address each with the appropriate party.

After the presentation, visit with the customer again and again to ensure that the solution elements are clear and that all their concerns and objections have been addressed. These visits help you build rapport that will enable open communication and create a team approach to solving their business needs. Furthermore, direct your efforts to address each objection head-on. This practice will display your integrity and also your commitment to validate the value of the solution for their organization. Although some may prefer a quick sale without many additional questions or objections, the process of working through objections leads to valuable dialogue and relationship-building.

Remember, you should not expect that you will always be able to offer a solution to an objection. Some objections will be easily overcome, while others are valid as they stand and you should simply agree that they cannot be addressed or changed by the solution. Only through detailed evaluation and analysis will you determine the credibility of each objection. Whatever the outcome will be, trying to discuss each of these items head-on is always the best approach. View the objections as additional opportunities to build relationships and learn more about your prospective customer.

Negotiate.
At this stage in the sales process, you have conducted your discovery sessions and defined the needs of the prospect. You have also married your solution elements to those identified needs so that it is clear in which ways the prospect will benefit from the solution. You have addressed all objections and clearly delivered the value of your solution. The next step in the sales process is the negotiation phase.

It is important to note that you can only start the negotiation phase once you have addressed all of the above. If you still have unanswered or unaddressed concerns on the table, then you will have a more difficult time during the negotiation phase. The more time and energy you put in to proving the solution, the more likely you will be to work towards a close.

For any negotiation, proper preparation is required. There must be time spent on a number of considerations so that you approach the interaction with a well-thought-out game plan. Some of these considerations are addressed in the questions below.

- What are your primary objectives or goals?
- What is your most ideal outcome?
- What is your minimal acceptable outcome?
- Does the solution presented fulfill all identified purchasing requirements?
- Does the proposed solution align with the budget discussed?
- What key elements of the solution resonated most with the prospect?
- How was the interaction throughout the sales process with the decision maker?
- What is your relationship like now with the decision maker?
- What will be your style or approach for the negotiation?
- Are there any historical occurrences that could have impact on the process?
- What is needed to ensure that the outcome is win-win for all involved?

Prior to your negotiation meeting, take time to write out answers to each of these questions. By organizing your thoughts, you will be most prepared for the actual negotiation. You may also uncover something that has been overlooked during the process.

When you are conducting the final solution elements and pricing, start with a discussion of what has been done thus far in the process. Remind the prospect of the interactions that you have shared and all that you have learned about their organization. This is an important step as they most likely have been through many meetings and have reviewed numerous solutions and solution elements. You should not expect that they will remember everything that they have learned or who they learned it from. This review offers confirmation on where you have been, and what you have covered in that time. This helps strengthen your value proposition. Additionally, it further differentiates you from your competition.

Inquire about any other areas that still may be unclear. Be prepared to put the final proposal review on hold so that you can clarify and discuss any topics needed. Once again, ensuring that the solution elements are clear and the value to the prospect is obvious will lead to fewer objections from the customer when discussing the final agreement.

When reviewing the proposal, the prospect may want to jump ahead and go directly to the pricing. If this is the case, deliver the pricing and then explain each of the solution elements that are included in the proposal. Leave nothing unaddressed. A detailed review of each of the elements will help to justify the final pricing proposed.

Once you complete your thorough review of all solution elements and pricing, shut up. Yes, I said shut up. It is at this point that you need to let the prospect digest what you proposed. It is also at this point that the meeting may sometimes get uncomfortable. If there is silence, you may feel pressure to fill the void with further explanation of your solution and how incredible it will be for them. Do not fall victim to this. Do not speak until the prospect speaks. This is a hard-and-fast rule. You cannot assume to know what the prospect is thinking. Wait and see how they react and what comes next.

Have confidence that the solution speaks directly to the needs of the prospect as uncovered in the discovery process. Have confidence that your pricing is fair for the value that it delivers. With that confidence, proceed with addressing whatever comes next. If the customer wants to cut price, then you can simply ask them what portions of the solution they want to remove and push into a future phase of the project. Perhaps they want it all for a lower price. If this is the case and you have more margin to spare, then you can lower the price. Either way, you will want to get some commitment from them throughout the process. Keep in mind that you have been getting small agreements and "yes" responses from them throughout the sales process. Small "yes" responses typically lead to a larger "yes" response, so keep asking for their commitment.

In the negotiation process, it is important for you to continue to validate your position. You can do this by utilizing the "If/Then" line of agreement questioning. This simply suggests that "if" you can do something for your prospect, "then" they can do something for you. For example, if the prospect asks, "Can you cut your pricing by 10 percent?" you can reply, "If I can get approval for an additional 10 percent, then will you be ready to sign the agreement today?"

Additionally, be prepared to say "no." Sometimes the prospect will simply ask for too much or ask for something that is beyond your control or ability to deliver. I suggest that when this occurs, you employ honesty and convey that you simply cannot do it. Saying "no" to a prospect is a very difficult thing to do, but when delivered at the right time, it can pay off in spades. Again, manage the interaction with integrity, professionalism, and a win-win objective. By doing this you can never go wrong.

The prospect's final decision may come quickly or in several steps. Your preparation will position you to act and react with confidence. Be prepared to leave the meeting without a final decision at times. There may be more information needed or the prospect may just need time to consider the final proposal. Either way, know that you have delivered the solution that is the best option for them.

Remember that although there may be typical stages in the negotiation process, employing creativity is always good practice. Think outside of the lines. Consider additional value-adds for the customer that may have significant impact on the transaction. These may come in many different forms and do not always have a cost associated. Ask yourself, can I spend more time with the prospect to explain functionality of the solution? Is there something else that I have access to at no or little cost that I can provide to the prospect to add value? Can I connect the customer with another resource or industry professional that will benefit their organization? If you put your thinking cap on, I'm sure you can get creative and add value to your proposed solution. This added value may just make the difference in the sale.

Your goal is to close the deal. Ask the prospect what it will take to get them to purchase. I know that this sounds simple, because it is. Listen attentively and see if you can give them what they are requesting. If you do not ask, then you will not know, or you will assume to know, which will not be effective. Once again, ask, ask, ask!

If you are in a sales environment where you are directly competing against another vendor in your industry, ask the customer if you can have a copy of the competitor's proposal. Sometimes the prospect will turn it over. Other times, they may tell you that they do not feel right about sharing it. If this is the case, I often request that the prospect just show this to me but not give me a copy. My justification for this is to ensure that the competitor's pricing was validated so that I could lobby for better pricing from my organization. In addition to validating the pricing, this also gives me the ability to see what is being offered from the competitor. With this information, I could validate if the solutions proposed were apples-to-apples, or if there were significant differences that created the pricing disparity. By collecting information on your competitors, you can stay up to date on their offerings and pricing, which in turn adds to your knowledge base and positioning as an industry expert.

When appropriate, deliver a Return-On-Investment (ROI) analysis with your proposal. An ROI document will justify the prospect's investment by pairing their value gained from the solution, often including the money they save, with their initial investment or purchase price. For example, previously I mentioned my interaction with Mike in the Needs Analysis section above. Mike found that the system he purchased added efficiencies to his food ordering process with his servers and kitchen staff. By doing so, there were fewer errors in the kitchen, thus providing weekly savings for his business. These savings were just one element that proved to him that he would recognize a return on his investment. The process of tallying up these savings and confirming their validity showed him that it was costing him money not to purchase a new solution. Of course, as mentioned earlier, his biggest win was the recapturing of time with his wife, which was "priceless."

As a reminder, a negotiation is open for interpretation. Sure, there are things that are commonly discussed or arranged in an agreement, but there is typically more on the table if you ask for it. For example, if you have ever purchased a car, then you are aware of the process of what happens after the test drive. The salesperson will sit you down in an office and price out their "best deal." They write the price per month down on a piece of paper and then push it over to your side of the desk. If you balk at the price, then the salesperson may ask you where it needs to be. You tell them, and then they need to leave the office to go "check with their manager."

This may go back and forth for a bit until you get the price you want. Does any of this sound familiar?

Let me tell you what happened the last time I purchased a car. First, I knew going in that my ideal monthly payment was about $500 per month. I had already researched and knew what I could get for that price and was prepared to purchase a car when I stepped on the lot. More importantly, I was also prepared not to. When I went to the dealership, I was greeted by a salesperson and told him the car that I was interested in.

We went through the standard pleasantries, conducted my test drive, and soon I found myself in his office where he "ran the numbers." He asked me about my monthly payment and I told him that I could not go over $400 (wink-wink), but if he could get me there then I would purchase today.

After his initial analysis, his proposed payment put me in somewhere around $530. I knew that I had a couple of rounds of negotiating with him before he needed to get his manager involved. He got me down to around $500 and then I asked him to check with his manager. When his manager came in I knew that he had the ability to get me down closer to the payment that I wanted. I also knew that after the negotiations with the manager were done, they would send me to the finance department who would try to sell me extra options and warranties that would push my price up again towards my ideal goal of $500. The manager and I went back and forth a few times. He would not offer the price that I wanted, so I told him that I would go to another dealership. I stood up, thanked him for his time, and started to walk out. He stopped me and asked me if he would give me a minute so that he could speak with his general manager. After another ten minutes, he came back and offered me a price of $419, which I said was good. Now off to finance.

The finance manager was a nice guy who took me through the options of warranties, alarm systems, protective coating, and other goodies that of course I wanted for my new car. They also offered in-house financing which would give me a bit more leverage, as I knew they controlled the interest rate and terms of the agreement. I worked with the finance manager, and we went through each of the options where I worked him down on each price. When all was said-and-done, he had my payment around $500, but I knew there was more on the table still. I asked him then to lower the interest rate so that I could get my payment down to $450 per month. Apparently, no one had ever negotiated this item down and he was at a loss for words. I told him that my payment could not go over $450 and asked him to talk to his manager. He came back in with the great news that he could get the interest rate lower and that my final payment would come in at $469.

Now I was jumping for joy on the inside, but I didn't let it show. I took a deep breath and was silent for a minute. I could feel how uncomfortable he was while he waited for me to respond. I then asked for one more thing. I said, "You know, I wash my car every other week at the local car wash. I usually spend about $10 per wash. Now I know that you guys have a car wash on site here at the dealership. If you allowed me to bring my car here to run it through your car wash every other week it would offset the $20 extra on my monthly car payment. It would also give me a chance to get to know your staff better. If you cover my car washes every month, then I'll sign." He paused and said, "Yes, we can do that."

So, at the end of the deal, I had the car that I wanted with all of the extras for $469 per month. I also covered my monthly car wash expense. I negotiated down the price, warranty, alarm, service package, and interest rate. I could have easily walked out with a much higher payment, but I asked for more, and was creative. The dealership still made money on the transaction, and I came out ahead. Win-win!

The point of this story is to remind you that as you negotiate your deals with your customer base, be creative and entertain all possibilities. Remember, everything is negotiable. Everything.

Take Order/Close.

Now that you have agreed to the terms of the transaction, it is time to take your new customer through the final documentation to close the order. This is yet another opportunity to strengthen your relationship with the customer. Make sure to review again each of the items that the customer is purchasing. Ask them if they clearly understand the solution, services, contract, payment terms, and any other associated items that would benefit from further explanation.

This is also your opportunity to ask the customer for a referral. You can simply pose the question: *Do you have any friends or business associates that you think could benefit from a solution or service like this?* If you have done your job correctly at this point, then they should be able to offer up a name or two which you can add to your warm leads list. We will touch on referrals more later, but for now, make this question part of your standard dialogue when you are signing contracts. Your customer will be on a "high" as they have bought in to your solution. This is the best time to ask them to share other contacts that they have which would want the same benefits.

Another valuable step after the close is the act of the project post-mortem. Wikipedia defines this as "a process, usually performed at the conclusion of a project, to determine and analyze elements of the project that were successful or unsuccessful." It is important to note that this can be done after a sales process that has resulted in a sale but also after a sales process that did not. Either way, you can learn from the interaction that you had with the customer. The best way to lead in to this post-mortem is to be as transparent as possible.

- **If you close the sale.** Mr. Customer, would it be okay if I asked you a few questions about the process that we went through? I am always trying to improve my work and your feedback would help me get better at what I do.
- **If you do not close the sale.** Ms. Customer, I understand that you chose a different solution or service based upon your needs. Would it be possible for me to ask you a few questions so that I could understand your how your final decision was made?

Next, the questions you ask can vary based upon your sales environment. Review the following questions to see how these would apply.

- How did our solution offering, or service compare to the competitors?
- What elements of the solution were most attractive to you? Why?
- Was the pricing in line and competitive with the other solutions that you considered? Will you elaborate on how the pricing was presented?
- Can you provide any feedback on our discovery process? Did I/we ask the right questions? Is there anything that I did not ask which I should have?
- Was the demonstration / presentation process and delivery on the mark? Was there anything that you felt was left out or not present? Were there any items that we should have spent more time on? What was the best / worst part of it?
- Overall, how would you rate our sales process? How could

we make it better?
- Is there anything that I could have done differently to earn your business?

Once you ask these questions, remember to listen and take notes. The feedback you get is golden and will help you improve if you let it. Take the feedback not as criticism, but as guidance. The best and most successful salespeople are open to feedback and use it to their advantage. In fact, the most successful people, regardless of profession, use the power of feedback to improve themselves regularly. Do not overestimate the value that this can bring you.

Remember that the sales process suggested above is only that—a suggestion. With that being said, you should make sure to use some version of this as each of these steps are necessary in a typical sales environment. Use this as a guide so that you will always know where you are in any opportunity. By knowing where you are, you can determine where you will go next. By following the process, you will move each lead through the process and have the best chances of success. In sales, it is said that you must plan your work, and then work your plan. Your plan is the sales process. Now go out and get to work.

Additionally, if you would like to review our INDENT sales process worksheets, visit our website at www.captureyourpower.com/resources.

takeaways & key ideas

1. Use the INDENT sales process.
2. By utilizing a sales process, you will always know exactly where you are in a sales opportunity and what the next step will be to move towards a close.
3. Prepare and rehearse your script for demo's, presentations, negotiations, and contract reviews.
4. Validate, empathize, restate, and ask again. Ask for what you want.
5. Deliver an ROI whenever possible. This justifies the customer's purchase.
6. Conduct a post-mortem on every deal, won or lost.

considerations

1. What are my five largest opportunities today? Where are they in the sales process described above?
2. How can I move them to the next stage in that process?
3. When was my last demonstration or presentation? Was I as

prepared as I should have been? What could I have done differently?

4. When was my last negotiation? Was I prepared? Did I follow a script? Did I exceed my minimal expectations?
5. How can I add value in a negotiation that can separate me from my competition?
6. Can I engage the last customer that I worked with and conduct a post-mortem? What could I have done differently?
7. Can I create an ROI for my products and services that I can use as a template for future opportunities?

THE 4 R'S OF SELLING

I have had a mentor for many years named Dan Harley who has taught me many things about sales and business. One of the most important was based on what he termed the "4 R's" of selling, expanded from Ivan Misner's "3 R's of Selling." The 4 R's stand for references, referrals, reorders or repeat customers, and relationships. Harley's opinion is that sales success can come from a number of different things: warm leads, cold calls, blue birds, luck, etc. But any substantial amount of success achieved will include a number of references, referrals, reorders, and strong relationships with your customer base and industry professionals. These are additional fundamentals that can have great significance in any sales environment. Let's take a moment to dig into each.

References and referrals.

If you have done your job correctly and have produced a happy and satisfied customer, then it is your duty to ask for references and referrals. Trust me, there is no better advertising or marketing than a happy customer who sings your praises to all that will listen. Creating a happy customer is hard work. You will need to make sure that you have done your best to deliver all aspects of the dream that you sold to them. Once you have worked hard to deliver this dream, you then can approach and ask them the following questions.

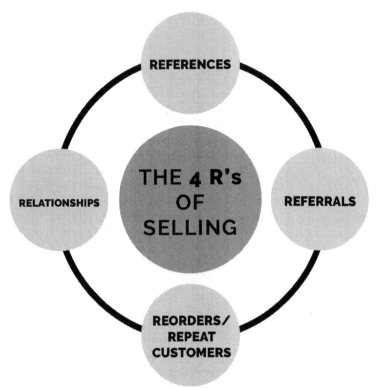

- Mr. Customer, would you be willing to write a reference letter that I can show to other potential customers who are considering our solution?
- Would you be open to taking a phone call from a prospective new customer and sharing your experience with them?
- Do you have any friends or business associates who you think would benefit from our solution?
- Would you provide the names and phone numbers of five of those contacts?

A customer can serve as both a referral source as well as a reference, although sometimes they may turn out to be only one or the other. Some customers may agree to write you a letter of recommendation, but do not want to be bothered by phone calls or inquiries from your new prospective clients. Others may not want to write a formal reference letter but are open to taking a phone call from a new prospective client. Still others may not be open to offering a formal recommendation, but may have insight as to friends, acquaintances, or business associates, who may have a need for your solution. Of course, the best option is to have a customer who will write you a letter of recommendation, offer to take phone calls or make a personal connection with new prospective clients on your behalf to validate the value of your solution, and will refer you to their friends, family, and business associates. This is the trifecta that will provide the most return for you.

Reorders or Repeat Customers.
Most product lines, solutions, and/or services have a life span attached to them. Your industry will have its own trends, but rest assured that your customer base will, at some time, be ready to purchase again. This may be due to a new model release, an upgrade, an add-on to enhance their current solution, or even due to the growth or evolution of the customer's business. When this need arises, it is your opportunity to engage and sell to this client again. We call this a reorder or repeat customer.

If you are in consulting, training, instruction, or a similar in-dustry and are selling yourself and your time as a service, then repeat customers or clients can be one of your most attractive market segments. These clients have already experienced the benefits of working with you and you do not need to spend as much time selling them on the value of your offer. Periodic engagements can serve to refresh and revive skills learned or information shared. Make sure to set calendar reminders to touch base with those who have contracted your services in the past. This is a familiar pond, rich in benefits, which you will want to fish from again in the future.

If you sell a product, service, or solution-based offering, then reorders can prove to be either really good or really bad. The really good part comes when a customer is excited about buying again and wants to engage with you on their next purchase. They come to you with additional inquiries and look to you for guidance and insight as they consider adding to their existing solution. They see you as a critical part of their success in this process.

The really bad part can come in a few different ways. This can happen when a customer feels like they are being forced to purchase more. They may approach the purchase with animosity and feel as if you, or your organization, have pushed them into a corner. This creates a very fragile sales environment, both for the customer and for you as well. Even if the customer does purchase the additional items, the process may leave them with a bitter taste and they may consciously or subconsciously carry resentment moving forward. This will weigh on the relationship and create possible opportunities

> ❝ *Whether winning or losing the sale, the only true loss is when you do not grow or learn from an interaction.*

for others to capture the business in the future.

The other "really bad" possibility is that a customer, realizing that they need to make a significant investment in their solution, may go out to review all available options and get bids from others in the marketplace. This can work against you in that the customer may be wooed by other solutions and may stray to the other side where the "grass is greener." If the solution needed is a full replacement, then you are more likely to have to approach the customer as if they were a brand-new prospect. This is typically the case in larger opportunities as well as anywhere public funds are being spent, as there is typically a requirement for multiple bids. Although this may lead the customer back to you in the end, it will undoubtedly be after you have worked to win-over the customer again and expended a large amount of effort in the process. This is also an opportunity for your competitors to expose any and all deficiencies in your solution, thus building up their own solution's value.

Regardless of the sales environment, many lessons can be learned from either a good or bad situation. Both can create an opportunity to educate that customer on the current market offerings. Additionally, both can reestablish your position as their trusted advisor, enable you to learn more about what the competition is offering, and show the customer that they had made the best choice to go with your solution in the first place. Most importantly, both can create an opportunity to strengthen your relationship and promote an atmosphere of open communication.

Now, it has been known to happen that when a long-time

customer is weighing their options in the marketplace, they may at the end of that process purchase a competitor's solution. This is, yet again, another learning opportunity. In this situation, you can analyze all of the events that transpired. Ask yourself what you could have done differently. What can you learn from this situation? Occasionally, the customer has been seduced by some aspect of the new solution, and when they find out it is not all that it was sold to be, they may come running back to you. If you stay professional through the entire process, you will come out winning in the end. Remember, take the high road. Whether winning or losing the sale, the only true loss is when you do not grow or learn from an interaction.

Relationships are most important.
So, you may be wondering how you can avoid the "really bad" situations mentioned above? How can you ensure that a customer jumps at the chance to serve as a reference for you? How can you encourage the new customer to open their contact list and hand over all sorts of referrals so that you can sell to everyone they know? Easy! Make sure that you have a strong relationship with them.

The relationship with the customer quickly becomes the most important "R" of the "4 R's," as all the others are dependent upon this. Developing your relationship with the customer will sometimes come naturally and organically, but other times will take a bit more effort. Most importantly, remain transparent and provide value to your customer. Relationships are built when you spend time on them. An easy way to justify spending time with the customer is to find a valid business reason (VBR) that is important to them. This can come through further exploration of a solution element or industry topic that is of

Capture Your Power in Sales and Business

interest to the customer. As a reminder, you are the industry expert here. Take opportunities to share with your customer relevant information that may include industry trends, new products or solutions, case studies, or legislation that may affect their business. Serve as a source of knowledge so that your customer will trust to come to you with any questions or inquiries in the future. By doing so, you will ensure that you are always in the loop as to what they are doing today and what their plans for the future are.

Another one of the most engaging activities that will strengthen any relationship is to eat a meal with them. This process of "breaking bread" typically will take the interaction to a new level of comfort and familiarity. As Michael Pollan writes in his book, *In Defense of Food: An Eater's Manifesto*, "The shared meal elevates eating from a mechanical process of fueling the body to a ritual of family and community, from the mere animal biology to an act of culture."

My recommendation is to suggest a meal before or after a meeting or presentation. In today's fast-paced world, many will not take the proper time out to plan their meals throughout their workday. If appropriate, suggest breakfast or coffee prior to an early morning meeting. Perhaps follow up a mid-morning meeting with an offer of lunch, or a mid-afternoon meeting with an early dinner. Invite your key contacts and any other decision makers or people of influence. The goal here is to take them out of their work environment and get to know them as people. People buy from people, and typically if there is no relationship, there is no sale.

In my career, I have had many occasions where I have needed

to travel to see clients in different cities across the country. On each trip, I did my best to fit in as many customer interactions as possible. For example, if I had a meeting or presentation with a customer in the morning, I would fly in one day early and see if there was a customer or prospect in town that I could take to dinner the night before. The next day, I would finish my meeting and then arrange a lunch for that customer and their team. I would try to organize another early dinner with a third customer or prospect and then schedule a late flight that night or an early flight the following morning. With a plan like that, I was able to engage multiple contacts during business hours and spend quality time with them during meals as well.

As I talk about eating meals with customers and prospects and spending time with them outside of their business environments, it is important to remind you that there is always the need to stay appropriate and ethical. We have all heard questionable stories of corporate funds being spent on "entertaining" customers and prospects. Make sure to stay within your organization's guidelines for entertaining customers, and if you have questions, refer to your management or executive leadership for guidance.

> **Get clients out of their work environment and get to know them as people. People buy from people, and typically if there is no relationship, there is no sale.**

Also, remember that although you are entertaining, you are still representing your organization, your brand, and yourself. If you consume alcohol during your meals, do so in moderation. I will admit, I am a big fan of wine and have been part of many customer engagements where we would take the time to collectively appreciate a great pairing, but again, do so in moderation. The last thing you want is to over-indulge with a customer or prospect and possibly compromise your opportunity to progress the business.

Other venues for customer bonding will vary depending on the industry you are in, but some other options could include a golf outing, a ball game, a visit to a competitor's site or store for competitive research, or a conference or industry event. Try not to overthink it. Once again, the goal is to get to know your customer. Seek to understand them as people, and approach this with sincerity and transparency. Learning about what makes them tick and getting a glance at their approach to life will undoubtedly provide further insight as to how they approach their business. Through additional understanding, you will be able to offer a more thorough and complete solution, and perhaps build incredible relationships and key contacts for the future.

1. Enhanced success is always accompanied by the 4 R's.
2. The most important of the 4 R's is Relationship.
3. Ask for references and referrals after closing a sale.
4. Every situation, regardless of if you win or lose the sale, is a learning opportunity.
5. Breaking bread with a customer changes a relationship.

1. Who in your customer base can serve as a referral? Have you asked them for a reference letter? How often do you see them or spend time with them?
2. What did you learn from your last reorder opportunity?
3. Who are the key players in your industry with whom you have a relationship? How can you make these stronger?
4. Which customers or prospects would you like to build a better relationship with? How can you incorporate this into

an action plan?
5. What valid business reason (VBR) can you offer to gain commitment from your prospect or customer to spend more time with you?

part 3

CAPTURING YOUR SALES SUCCESS

USING TECHNOLOGY

We live in a time of extraordinary technology. We have cars that can drive and park themselves. We have phones that have more computing power than the first spaceship that went to the moon. We have tools upon tools upon tools that help us with our everyday lives. All this technology is in place to help us with our daily tasks. Technology makes our life easier by adding conveniences and efficiencies to our daily routine. It can also help us remember important dates and information that we can access later. Let's face it, with over 50,000 thoughts a day, we all could use a little help with organization and reminders from time to time.

In this chapter, I will focus on some technological tools that can assist you in your daily sales efforts. Note that there are too many to list in one chapter, but I will share with you some thoughts on items that have added to my productivity and success. Most of these can be used on your smartphone or computer or both. Some are free, and some take a small investment. Either way, it will be worth it to you in the long run to research and acquire the tools, then use them daily.

Let's start with your phone. Chances are that you are one of the 2 billion smartphone users on the planet. Although most people use these smartphones to make phone calls, video chat, or share pictures and videos, there are an abundance of applications available on your smartphone that you can use daily to help you organize and manage your business. Let me mention some of my favorites.

SOCIAL MEDIA APPS

Facebook.

As Facebook is approaching nearly 2 billion users, the chances are that your customers have a profile that you can find and review. Even without being a "friend," you can look up Facebook profiles and gain important information on a person or business easily. You can learn what they are up to, what they like, and how they feel about your brand. Facebook profiles are free to set up, so you can set one up for yourself, but do so cautiously. You will want to consider what your customers will be able to see about you. Everything you post online has the possibility of being seen by anyone. Ask yourself, how will my Facebook activity affect my business? Do I want my customers to see this? Perhaps you should start a separate Facebook business page or review your personal profile to make sure that it represents you appropriately.

Also, if you use a business Facebook page, make sure to space out your posts and only post items that add value for your customers. Do not fall in to the habit of posting every hour with meaningless info. This does not do any favors for your business. Also, use pictures and video when possible as these mediums are proven to stimulate more interaction. As with any of the social media apps mentioned, start slowly and build up from there. This can become one of your best tools if used correctly.

Instagram.

This is another free application that enables you to share pictures and video. This can integrate with your Facebook application and enables you to post to both applications at once. Instagram currently has approximately 500 million active users and is growing rapidly. As with Facebook, you can follow other's profiles on this application to stay up to date with pertinent activity related to your industry.

Twitter.

Some would say that the hype of Twitter has faded, but there are still over 300 million users currently. This application enables the user to post 280 characters to their followers and can provide additional insight and info on user activity. My suggestion, start a Twitter account and follow those that you want to do business with. You will learn a bunch.

Pinterest.

Hi-resolution pictures can be shared on this site and can go viral quickly. Once again, follow those who you want to do business with. Also, if appropriate, use this platform to post pictures of new products that you offer.

YouTube.

YouTube has over 1 billion active users and is the second largest search engine, so you will want to use this frequently. As YouTube is owned by Google, random searches will show videos more often and can provide links to content that can help with research of others as well as help promote your products or services. As mentioned above, you can link You-Tube to Facebook, Instagram, and Twitter, so that one post can touch all applications simultaneously. This saves you time with multiple posts and provides the best opportunity to reach your customer base.

LinkedIn.
As a business professional, LinkedIn has proved to be the best application for me to connect with other professionals. This application enables you to create a professional profile with work experience, certifications, referrals, and any other related information for all to see. It also enables you to connect with your "network" and with extended networks, giving you the opportunity to grow your reach with other business professionals. There is also the opportunity to post to your network, one that I have used to offer commentary and insight on a number of topics. LinkedIn has nearly 500 million business users in over 200 countries and is the best application to mix business and social media.

Tumblr.
This application offers the ability to share photos, GIFs, videos, music, chats, links, and text and has approximately 50 million active users. This application may not be as popular as YouTube, but still has a presence and can integrate with all the apps listed above.

Yelp.
Valuable information can be learned from Yelp through customer reviews. If you are a business owner, you can build a strategic plan to acquire positive reviews. If you are researching a business, you can see what others are saying about the

business and its offerings. Yelp can also assist with advertising campaigns for small businesses.

PRODUCTIVITY APPS

JotNot.
This application enables you to use your smartphone to capture an image with the camera, convert it to a PDF, and email it to anyone. Straightforward, and incredibly valuable.

Dropbox.
You can upload, store, and share files with this free application. There is also a business Dropbox available that gives you the ability to create user groups and provides unlimited storage. Google Drive is another option with similar functionality. This tool is a must for those on the go.

Google Hangout.
This is a free video-conferencing tool that enables you to have up to 10 users on a conference call at one time. Users must have a Google account, but the quality of the application is top-notch. There are many video-conferencing tools to choose from, so make sure to add one to your tool belt for easy access.

Google.
I know that this may be obvious, but Google is by far the best search engine available today. If you want to know anything about anything, Google it. Start every inquiry here and use different terminology for different results. Any industry professional today will have some sort of web presence. Google is your front door to the information warehouse. Open it and see what's inside.

Wrike.
This is a free project management tool. You can create projects and user groups, assign tasks with reminders and calendar deadlines, and more. This integrates with Dropbox as well for file sharing. Other notable solutions in this space are Basecamp, Asana, and Trello. The point is, use one.

Wunderlist.
This app lets you organize and share your to-do lists. This is basically your "reminders" app that is already part of the Apple operating system but offers a few more bells and whistles.

Tripit.
If you travel, this app serves as a travel organizer. This will organize all elements of your itinerary (hotel, car, flight, dinner reservations) in one place. You can also forward your travel emails to build an itinerary. This is very useful and convenient.

Adobe Creative Cloud.
The Adobe suite has many different applications that can assist you in what you do. I have used PhotoShop to create marketing brochures and edit graphical content when necessary. PhotoShop can be a bit intimidating initially, but with a few tutorials and a little practice, you can pick up the basics quickly. Also, the Creative Cloud offers Adobe Acrobat which you can use to create and edit PDF files. This is a must if you are preparing contracts regularly. There is a plethora of additional tools here to help you create, illustrate, animate, and design all sorts of things. You can add these on for a monthly charge and have the software hosted in the cloud. This is a justifiable business expense.

Microsoft OneNote.

This application that is typically included in a Microsoft Office Suite is a program for free-form information gathering and multi-user collaboration. It gathers users' notes (handwritten or typed), drawings, screen clippings, and audio commentaries. This application also enables you to share notes with other OneNote users over the Internet or a network. This is an incredible tool for aggregating all of your information in one place. An alternative to this application is Evernote.

Your standard iPhone, Android, or other smartphone device.

It is important to note that a standard smartphone has tools that you will use daily as well. All have built-in calculators, access to Wi-Fi, cameras, text messaging, and more. Configure your device to have these items on the home screen and enable quick links or shortcuts so that you can get to them easily. Also, just as I advised that you rehearse your sales presentation before delivery, you should also your practice accessing these smartphone items quickly, as you may need to do so in front of a customer.

Side note: make sure your screen saver is appropriate. A picture of your children is much better for a customer to see when you pull out your phone than a modeling pic of a Kardashian backside (for example).

EMAIL, CALENDAR, AND CONTACTS

Microsoft Office 365.

Microsoft Office is a suite of products that incorporates email (Outlook), calendar, and contact software all in one package. MS

Office is an industry standard that has many add-ins to make the organization of these items fluid and efficient. Another benefit for this is that you can use it on a PC or Mac.

For many years, I used Outlook only for emails and to manage my task list as it was all integrated in a single application. I would move emails inquiries directly into contacts and create follow-up items with reminders set in my calendar. It was seamless. I also had the ability to connect to a corporate account using the Microsoft Exchange server which provided additional benefits. If you have access to this, my suggestion would be to use it. If you do not have an exchange server, you can still use Outlook along with a Google calendar and contacts that all integrate to your smartphone device.

The main goal is to have access to your emails, contacts, calendar, tasks, and project management both on your smartphone and on your desktop, laptop, or tablet. Having all of this at your fingertips anywhere at any time will ensure that you are always prepared to handle anything that comes up. Also, this integration will help you make more efficient use of your workday. Additional benefits to MS Office are the availability of PowerPoint, Word, and Excel. Although Apple has their own versions of these (Keynote, Pages, and Numbers), the MS Office staples are the industry standard and will give you the best foundation. Furthermore, these various file formats can be imported and exported through various applications as necessary.

Today, there are many different worthy applications available and you have many choices. It does not matter any longer if you use a PC or a Mac as both platforms have made efforts to play nice and offer integration. For me personally, I used all PC products religiously for over twenty years and was extremely successful doing so. In the last five to seven years however, I have added a host of Apple-based products and have conducted my own testing. Today, I am most comfortable using a Mac laptop with MS Office 365. I use the email engine of Outlook, but sync contacts and calendar through my iCloud. There could definitely be more thorough integration, but I have made it work for my businesses. The moral of the story: Find what works for you and become an expert on the applications that you use. The more familiar you are with these tools, the better you will be at using them.

EQUIPMENT

In addition to the software that you use, you will want to make sure to have a few staple tools in your laptop bag to ensure you are prepared for your daily tasks. Some may be necessary for your sales environment, and some may not, but all have extreme value in the right situation.

External Storage Device.
Make sure to purchase an external storage device that you can use to back up your laptop or desktop files. This is best when it is done automatically on a fixed schedule so that you don't have to remember to do it. Both a PC and Mac OS will have automatic back-up scheduling that can be programmed ahead of time. An external storage device of 1 or 2 terabytes should be more than sufficient to back anything up and can be purchased for under $100. If you are paranoid, you can purchase two of them and have one back up the other. I have done this in the past, but when I started using Dropbox

business I found that this was not necessary. Today I have all pertinent information on my laptop, on my external device, and on Dropbox. If you have ever lost your information due to a device crashing, then you know how painful the recovery process can be.

USB Flash Drive.
It is useful as well to have a USB flash drive available in your bag. If you have a file that you want to share with someone but do not have Internet access, you can use the flash drive to transfer it quickly. Additionally, I would always recommend putting your PowerPoint presentation on a flash drive prior to any presentation. I have seen too many times where a laptop fails, or a file is corrupt, or a situation requires that different equipment to be used. These meetings are far too important to have a single point of failure. Back up your work, and again, be prepared for any situation.

Slide Advancer/Laser Pointer.
This item plugs into a USB port on your computer and gives you the ability to press a button on a handheld device that will advance your slides during a presentation. Most also have a built-in laser pointer so that you can spotlight areas of importance as necessary. This tool enables you to be mobile while presenting and releases you from being chained to your laptop. One more thing, make sure to pack extra batteries for this device. Typically, they take one AAA battery, and a spare will not take up any room at all in your bag.

Converter cables.
If you are presenting regularly, you may want to invest in a converter cable that enables you to connect your laptop to

a TV or monitor. Based upon your laptop ports, this may be an HDMI to HDMI, HDMI to RCA, Display port to HDMI, or a combination of VGA and audio ports on older devices. Do yourself a favor and visit your local electronics store to inquire as to how to connect your laptop to an external monitor or TV. Most new TVs will have an available HDMI port, but older ones may only have RCA ports available.

Back-up chargers.
I know this seems obvious, but there is nothing worse than working your tail off preparing for a presentation or contract negotiation only to find that your device has no charge. This showing of not being prepared is not something that you want to display in front of the customer. This may not be a cheap purchase, but again, if it saves you one time then it is worth the cost.

Extension cord.
Really? Yes. They are small and cheap and can come in so handy when you do not have enough plugs or just cannot get close enough to the wall outlet. Trust me on this one. You will thank me later.

Ethernet cable.
Although Wi-Fi is available in most places today, the speed and reliability of a Wi-Fi network will never match a hard-wired connection. If you are trying to access something online or cloud-based, then you will want the most reliable and fastest network connection possible. A 3 or 6-foot cable will do the trick.

FUTURE APPLICATIONS AND TOOLS

In addition to using available technology to help you today, you will also want to stay up-to-speed on new applications and solutions as they launch. An easy way to do this is to subscribe to a technology blog, podcast, or magazine that can keep you informed on new solutions as they hit the market. Simply search for "technology for business" on Google and select the most appropriate topic for your needs. This research will not only help you to maintain your efficiency but will also make you an expert on industry tools. As your business grows, you will need to continually find new ways to work smarter. This information will aide you in that process.

Finally, as you entertain new solutions, make sure that you ask the right questions to ensure they will work for you.

- Does this integrate with my current platform? Is there training available?
- Does this company have support staff available for me in case I need it?
- Are there reviews from other users that I can reference?
- Is there a trial version of this application that I can preview?

Your goal is to continue to find tools that support further success. Remember, work smarter, not harder. Embrace technology and make it work for you. By doing so, you can climb to new levels of success that have never been reached before.

Bonus Tip!
Technology is incredible, but you always need to be prepared for anything, so have a pen and a notebook available at all

times. This option is not dependent on an Internet connection, battery charge, or operating system. My recommendation is to always carry with you multiple pens, highlighters, and a notebook with numbered pages. You use this to capture everything and then archive these books at the end of the year. All written documentation can be transferred as necessary via OCR (optical character recognition) to your computer. The OCR is a functionality of the Adobe Creative Cloud mentioned above, and there are many different options on the market today at little or no cost. Or, for a quick hack, pull out your phone, snap a picture of the notes, and email it to yourself to ensure that you keep it safe and handy.

takeaways & key ideas

1. Technology can make you more efficient and enable further success.
2. Social media is your friend. Embrace it and figure out how to use it to your advantage.
3. Ask your friends and colleagues for their favorite three apps that they use for business. See what they say and if they can work for you.
4. Leverage "the cloud" to back up, store, and share your information. Sync your devices and feel the power of immediate access to your information, anytime and anywhere.
5. If you find someone whose "propeller" spins faster than yours, ask them for help and guidance.
6. Your smartphone in your pocket or purse has more power than the first space shuttle. Ask an expert how you can use it in more ways.
7. Sign up for newsfeeds or blogs where you can always stay abreast on what technology is coming next.

considerations

1. What technology are you using today? Is it doing everything you want it to do in your business?
2. What processes or procedures can you automate with technology?
3. Of your circle of friends and colleagues, who uses technology most efficiently? Can you take them to lunch and ask them what guidance they can give you to use more of it in your business?
4. Are you prepared when the worst-case scenario happens? Do you have your files backed up? Do you have your back-up tools in your laptop bag?
5. How is your social media profile? Would you hire you after looking at your Facebook, Instagram, or LinkedIn account? Can you make these more attractive or appropriate for public consumption?

TIME MANAGEMENT

"Time management" is a term used very often in both professional and personal settings. We are all seeking new ways to save time, manage time, steal time, borrow time, and maximize time. Time has been called many things: the great equalizer, the greatest value, our most precious commodity, and our wisest investment. Regardless of how you reference it, the truth is that time happens. It passes, and you don't get it back. It is the same for everyone, regardless of race, culture, sex, religion, socioeconomic class, or status. We all have the same 24 hours a day, and the only thing we have control over is how we use it.

We typically relate time and achievement to productivity. We may think that people who get more done in the same amount of time achieve more and get better results. This has some truth in it, but I will remind you that just getting lots of things done does not always equate to achieving more or producing better results. Many fall victim to meaningless busy work. The time you use should be applied to efforts that can produce maximal returns. We will touch on this subject more in the coming chapters, but for now let's agree that to be successful, you will need to ensure that you are planning, tracking, and reviewing how you use your time. This is where we will begin.

If you are like me, your daily life has too many activities to remember without help. In fact, by lunchtime today I will have spent time writing, exercising, waking kids and getting them to school, and conducting a staff meeting. This is just the first half of my day, and just one day of my week. So how do I plan and track my time? Here is what works for me—and some additional thoughts that may have some significance for you as well.

Daily Calendar.
This may seem obvious, but you should log all your appointments in your daily calendar. Ideally, this would be a calendar that you carry with you wherever you go so that you can refer to it when necessary. Smart phones are an ideal convenience as you always have these with you. Additionally, you can have all your information (contacts, emails, and calendar) in one device. You can also use the built-in tools of the phone for convenience and efficiency. For example, if you own an Apple iPhone, you can simply ask Siri (the automated iPhone assistant) to schedule an appointment for you on a certain day. In fact, Siri can set reminders, schedule appointments, read text and email messages, make phone calls, transcribe voicemails, and more. You may need some help with how to use this functionality, but a local visit to your local wireless store or Apple genius bar at

> **To be successful you will need to ensure that you are planning, tracking, and reviewing how you use your time.**

the Apple store will get you all set up to go.

Most other smart phone devices today have a built-in assistant to offer similar capabilities. (Microsoft has Cortana, Amazon has Alexa, and Google has Assistant.) Additionally, your smart device provides the benefit of syncing or "mirroring" your information in real time with your computer or email engine. The marriage of these devices gives you the ability to be anywhere and still have the ability to access all of your information. The goal with time management is to utilize time in the most efficient manner possible. The technology is there to use, so use it.

If you are like my wife who prefers to write down each appointment in pencil in a daily calendar, then the most important thing to do is to ensure that it is with you all the time so that you have it available to reference. Select a tool that is easy to transport and work with regularly and make sure to tie a pencil to it so that you have something to write with. A pencil is needed as it has the ability to erase when an appointment time is modified. While you are at it, make sure to have a pencil sharpener handy (or a mechanical pencil with extra lead), so that you do not have any excuse not to write an appointment in your calendar.

What do we put in our calendar?
Simply put, you will log everything you spend your time on to your calendar. Of course, this includes all of your appointments, but it also includes free or personal time, planning time, follow-up time, and pop-ups (unexpected things that come up and take your time). Each of these areas are of importance and deserve to have their own blocks of time allocated to them.

Time Management

By blocking this out for each category, we are protecting this time to ensure that we actually get to them.

Free or personal time.
Free or personal time can include a number of different items that you may or may not be in the habit of adding to your calendar. Workouts, meditation, massage, trips to the grocery store, reading, cleaning, and other daily duties may make up some of these areas that deserve to be on your calendar. You may be asking yourself, "Do I really need to schedule my free time?" In short, the answer is absolutely. These items are added to your calendar to ensure that you spend time doing them. Additionally, if they are not added to your calendar and you find yourself doing them anyway, then chances are that you are sabotaging other activities that deserve your effort.

Ideally, planning time should be on the calendar at the start or end of each day. Personally, I have found that using both time blocks works best for me. At the end of each day, I reassess my work and accomplishments for the current day and then plan the next one. At the start of the next morning before I begin the day, I review the list or schedule with a fresh set of eyes, confirm that I have all of my daily priorities listed, and modify as appropriate. I will then follow the same cycle at the end of the day with a review of what I have accomplished as I plan for the following day.

As mentioned earlier, successful people plan their work and then work their plan. The planning removes the guesswork and will steer you towards action without wasting time trying to figure out what to do next. Time management is not possible without planning. Although some things cannot be planned down to the detail, other things can and should be planned. Laying the groundwork in advance gives you a starting place upon which you can grow from. The mere process of planning will serve to give you an advantage as you have thought out scenarios and situations ahead of time and are ready to act when prompted.

If you have a territory or assigned geographical area, it is important that you meticulously segment your area and chart your prospecting each day in an effort to ensure maximum coverage. Consider planning the week before and assigning different prospecting areas to each day. You can plan what time you will start, which street or list you will start on, and how you will proceed from there. You can also plan your breaks and lunches to ensure that you can engage with any possible prospects as a patron of their establishment.

If you wake each morning with a plan in place, then you will maximize your productivity. Of course, you can modify this as necessary, but you will never have any doubt about where to start. If you want to take it one step further, you can even pick out your clothes that you plan on wearing the night before and lay them out. By doing so, you will be ready to wake up and jump right in to your day. Is this overkill? Perhaps—but you will find that it starts you off each morning with a detailed guide that will lead you to a successful and productive day.

Successful people plan their work, then work their plan.

Follow-ups.

Inevitably, your efforts during each day will produce actions that you will need to react to. Scheduling time at some point during the day to follow up on the day's or week's new activity is necessary to move your prospects and business along. Keep in mind that you can create all sorts of new leads, but if you do not review and qualify these in an effective way, they will not generate closed sales. This practice will take on different forms throughout your career, but the allocation of having a block of "follow-up" time will always be necessary. Make this a habit and stick with it.

Pop-ups.

Pop-ups are items that come up during your day that are unexpected. Not all pop-ups deserve your time, but some most certainly do. As business changes so rapidly from day to day, even the best-planned schedule can be thrown off by pop-ups. Allocating time on your daily calendar for such contingencies can save you from losing an entire day to an unexpected turn of events. If no pop-ups occur, then you can reallocate that time to your next priority.

Work smarter not harder.

This phrase is referenced often, and for good reason. There is something to be said for constant review of the way you are getting things done. Standard company protocols and procedures are necessary and good to have, but occasionally they need to be rethought and reevaluated to ensure that the way they are being completed is the best way to do them. Working smarter is about using the knowledge that you have today to improve upon the work that was planned with yesterday's knowledge. It is about utilizing new technology, services, or solutions and combining them with any new information and experience, so you can achieve the highest level of efficiency. While approaching your daily tasks, ask yourself these questions.

- Is this the best way that this can be done?
- Are others doing it differently?
- If I tried to do it differently, how would the outcome change?
- What tools are available to assist with this that I am not using today?

Remember, doing the same thing over and over will not produce different results. Try something new, innovative—risky even—and you may be surprised by the outcome.

What is your time worth?
Whether you are just starting out or you already have a thriving business, evaluating where and how you spend your time is paramount. We all have mundane tasks that need to be completed daily, but the question I pose is "Do they need to be completed by me?" Some things on your list will need to be completed by you, as you are the only one with the knowledge and familiarity to complete them. But, I'll ask again in a different way: can you train someone else to do these items?

> 66 *Working smarter is using the knowledge that you have today to improve upon the work that was planned with yesterday's knowledge.*

Time Management

Successful people realize that they cannot do everything themselves. They delegate what they can to others to produce increased results. The powers and capabilities of a team will always outweigh the powers and capabilities of a single person. Help is all around you, and it is up to you to utilize it.

So how can you decide if a task is worth your time? An easy way to start is by defining your hourly rate. Take the amount of money you make in a year and break that down by a monthly average, then a weekly average, then a daily average, then an hourly rate. For example, if you make $100,000 a year, and work an average of 40 hours a week, we can divide $100,000 by 2000 (40 x 50 weeks) that gives us an average hourly rate of $50. Now you may overthink this and consider taxes, vacations, time off, and other holiday pay, but we are looking for an average here. If you think this is too high, then take it down a bit. The goal here is to define an average hourly rate that you can use as a measuring stick against anything that you spend time on. With this hourly rate, you can determine if you should delegate or hire out or do it yourself.

Question: Should I pick up my dry cleaning?
Answer: Can I delegate or hire someone for less than $50 to do it?

Question: Should I spend the next two hours completing these contracts?
Answer: Can I have someone else do them efficiently, and cut them into the deal at less than $50 per hour so that I can move on to the next sale?

Question: Should I make follow up calls on prospect leads?

Answer: Can I train a junior rep to take this over or hire an assistant and offer them compensation at less than $50 per hour?

Tim Ferriss writes in his book *The 4-Hour Workweek* about the need to eliminate, automate, and delegate. Eliminate any tasks that are not worth doing or that do not contribute to the accomplishment of your goals, automate any procedures or tasks that can be automated, and delegate any tasks that can be handed off to someone else. The mere process of considering items to delegate, eliminate, and automate will train your brain to filter through the daily workload. This paves the way for you to allocate your time to the most essential actions to propel your business.

An Alternative Approach.
My work as a business coach and consultant has exposed me to many examples of how to add efficiencies to your business. I can recall working with a client a few years back who was a very successful real estate agent named Jennifer. Jennifer had spent years seeding the market and her hard work had paid off. She found herself in a predicament though as she had too much business to handle and not enough time to do it. She was in a position that few others had ever reached in her company and was pushing the limits of her capabilities inside of the corporate structure that existed at that time. She was responsible for finding new clients, qualifying them as valid prospects, taking them through the sales cycle, moving them through closing contracts, and following up afterwards to ensure that the purchasers received all that they had envisioned. There were so many steps in the process that just one deal could become all-consuming: and she had fifteen to twenty

deals in some phase of the sales cycle at any given time. She simply could not keep up and had to find a new way to get things done.

In our time working together, Jennifer realized that she was extremely fortunate to have so much business but knew nevertheless that she needed a new strategy. We also recognized that other agents were not as busy and were very interested in how she was achieving all of her success.

We constructed a plan for her to begin to bring in other junior agents on smaller deals where she could mentor them on the process and also task them with some of the related responsibilities. By doing so, she would compensate them for their time, offer them training and guidance throughout the process, and work more efficiently by handing them the bulk of the time-consuming duties. Furthermore, she aligned herself with an inside sales agent who took over her contract submissions. This inside agent was given a small piece of every deal that he worked on, and he was ecstatic as this gave him the opportunity to make more money than ever before.

By being creative, Jennifer created an environment where everyone benefitted. Her team made more money, they received more guidance and coaching from her, and the entire office enjoyed an abundance of new business. Furthermore, this gave her the opportunity to spend more time on the bigger opportunities that fed the cycle more and more. Once she implemented these processes, her personal income nearly doubled, and she surpassed every sales record company-wide that had been set up to that point.

Find Your 20%.
You have no-doubt heard of the rule of 80/20, also referred to as the *Pareto Principle*. This principle was named after the Italian economist Vilfredo Pareto, who observed that 80% of income in Italy was received by 20% of the Italian population. He further noticed a similar occurrence in multiple areas of his environment and concluded that most of the results in any situation are determined by a small number of causes. Let me rephrase that. *The majority of your results come from a small portion of your activity.* This has application not only in business, but in every area of your life. Let's explore.

> Identify the 20% that is producing the best results in any area of your life. Once you have defined that, plan to do more of that, and plan to do that first everyday.

In Business.
In the business world, there are many occurrences of the 80/20 ratio. We find this across multiple industries and verticals, in macro and micro settings, and throughout all branches and departments inside organizations. Here are some further examples of how this rule can apply as mentioned by quality management thinker Dr. Joseph Juran.

- 80% of problems can be attributed to 20% of causes
- 80% of a company's profits come from 20% of its customers
- 80% of a company's complaints come from 20% of its

customers
- 80% of a company's profits come from 20% of the time its staff expends
- 80% of a company's revenue comes from 20% of its products
- 80% of a company's sales are made by 20% of its sales staff

To break this down further and personalize it, I will replace the word "company" with "your individual."

- 80% of your *individual* problems can be attributed to 20% of your causes
- 80% of your *individual* profits come from 20% of your customers
- 80% of your *individual* complaints come from 20% of your customers
- 80% of your *individual* profits come from 20% of the time you spent

In Your Personal Life.
If you conduct an experiment and take notice of how often the 80/20 rule comes into play in your personal life, you may be surprised by the results.

- 80% of free time with friends is spent with only 20% of your group of friends
- 80% of income is spent on 20% of your monthly bills (rent, mortgage, car payment)
- Even nearly 80% of your free time weekly comes up during 20% of the week (the weekends!)

Regardless of what the actual percentage breakdown may

be, generally speaking, the rule of 80/20 will ring true. So, how do you capitalize on this information? Easy! Concentrate on the 20%. Place your focus on the things that provide the most return. Allocate time on your calendar for these things and treat them as your main priority. If there is one customer that provides 80% of your revenue, then make sure that you are devoting appropriate time to them. If 20% of your funnel has the best opportunity to close, then work that 20% first. I will not complicate the topic with many more examples. Simply put, define what your 20% is that is working best to produce results in any area of your life. Once you have defined that, plan to do more of that, and plan to do that first every day.

Avoid Distractions.

Distractions are everywhere. They can sneak up on you and throw you off course quickly. These can come in many forms in any venue and can sabotage your plan or schedule without you knowing it. In an office setting, an interruption by a neighbor or colleague can pull you away. An email ping on your computer can lead you down a rabbit's hole for hours if you let it. A Facebook alert can coax you to browse through updates for an entire afternoon. The trick is to eliminate the distractions. Make sure that you are in a work area where you can be most productive. Turn off your alerts, silence your phone, and close your door. Put on headphones for silence if necessary and put up a sign stating that you are not to be interrupted. Move to an environment where it is conducive to be productive. Use the out-of-office functionality on your email so that others are not expecting an immediate response. Check emails only during scheduled times daily and resist the temptation of reacting instantly to new requests. Distractions will throw you off course if you let them. Your job is to take them out of the equation so that you can stay on course.

Time is a tool. It is also a precious gift. There will be occasions where you use it wisely. There will be other occasions where you use it frivolously. Both have their place, as long as you are aware and accept the consequences. No matter how you choose to use your time, commit to it and do it whole-heartedly. Use the guidelines discussed above as simply that—guidelines. The goal with using time in business is to ensure that you are staying efficient through being productive. Ask others what works for them. Through investigation, analysis, and experience you will be able to chart your own course and come up with a system that works for you.

takeaways & key ideas

1. Use a daily calendar to schedule all appointments and obligations. Keep it with you at all times on your phone or in a separate journal.
2. Schedule free time and personal time to ensure that you protect it.
3. Schedule time to review and revise your daily plans.
4. Schedule both follow-ups and pop-ups.
5. Work smarter and more creatively to get more done.
6. Determine what your time is worth, and delegate what you can.
7. The majority of your success comes from a small portion of your efforts.
8. By concentrating on the 20% of what produces the most results, you can recognize further success.
9. 20% of the workforce in your organization produces 80% of the success.
10. Create reminders in your work space and home to keep you focused on the 20%.
11. Create an environment to work where there are no distractions.

considerations

1. Am I currently scheduling time blocks for all areas of my life (work time, exercise, personal time, planning time, follow-ups, and pop-ups)?
2. Am I setting myself up for a successful day by planning the night before?
3. Are there ways that I can work differently or more creatively that can save time and add efficiency?
4. What can I automate, delegate, or eliminate today?
5. What activity do I do that produces the majority of my success, sales, or results?
6. How can I incorporate more of this defined activity in each day?
7. Where does most of my enjoyment at work come from? How can I do more of this?
8. Where does most of the enjoyment in my personal life come from? How can I do more of this?
9. What common distractions can I avoid in my work day? What typically pulls me off course throughout my day?
10. What percentage of my day is spent on strategy? Planning? Task management? Meetings? Paperwork or administrative duties? Is this percentage ideal? Does it support an environment to achieve my goals?

ASKING THE RIGHT QUESTIONS

In sales and business in general, we have an incredible opportunity to learn from those we interact with daily. We can learn about customers and their business, industry, concerns, outlook, and more. We can dig deeper and learn about their goals, aspirations, and desires. We also have the opportunity to learn about ourselves through the process. This learning can only come from inquiry, but not all inquiry is the same. The power of learning comes through the process of asking the right questions at the right time, and then listening attentively and taking detailed notes to ensure that we retain the information.

Asking the right questions will produce the best information possible. Asking the right question at the right time may produce a game-changing conversation that can change your relationship and accelerate the pace of the sale. So how do you know which question to ask and when to ask it? Let's start with the basics first and move on from there.

Salespeople get paid to uncover new sales opportunities. We are investigators of a sort, working diligently to determine who could be a potential customer; what product, service or solution that potential customer can use; how they can use it;

when they would use it; and most importantly, why they would need or want to use it. These are the basis of our initial inquiry and build the foundation of information needed to guide us through the sales process.

Although you now have the introductory questions to ask, it is important to note that there is a bit of style that needs to be employed to make this process as natural as possible. I have been witness too many times to sales reps or agents failing to engage a new business or customer. Often, they only succeed in fumbling over their words and creating a very awkward situation. This typically does not lead to anything good. The art of asking questions comes through your natural ability to carry a conversation. It is through this conversation that you create an environment where the prospect or customer feels safe and secure so that information can be shared.

> ❝ *The success of a salesperson is directly connected to the depth of the quetsions they ask.*

If you are still unsure about how to engage, I would recommend that you practice out loud with a partner or friend. Be conscious if you are asking open-ended or closed-ended questions. An open-ended question creates opportunities for sharing information. A close-ended question can be answered with a one-word response and does not leave room for further elaboration. As an example, if I asked, "Did you like that movie?", you could simply answer "yes". This is an example of a closed-ended question. If I were to ask you "What did you like about that movie?", it would be an open-ended question which would stimulate further conversation. As you practice your questioning in your sales environment, you will familiarize yourself with standard responses or objections that may come up frequently. Only through practice and constant interaction can you become more fluid at this.

Remember, you have been engaging in conversations throughout your whole life. You have years and years of experience under your belt. Now you may have had less experience discussing the topic of your product, solution or service, but you still know how to talk. You still know how to introduce yourself. You still know how to smile. These are the basics. Start by initiating a conversation where you introduce yourself, say hello, and ask how they are doing. This is half the battle. Through this process, you will become more comfortable with yourself and promote an atmosphere where others will want to engage with you.

Seek to understand.
As you are gathering your information, you goal is to seek to understand your customer or confirm your understanding from your research. Your job is to continue to ask questions to stimulate the sharing of information. You are trying to uncover not only all of the facts of the opportunity, but also all of the emotions that accompany the facts. It is not merely the mechanics of how something is being done that is important. What becomes equally important are the emotions created and experienced through that process. To truly understand the customer, you must work to unravel each of these items with them. Surprises and epiphanies may arise along the way. This

is normal. As you invite someone to speak about themselves and their business out loud, interesting things happen and discoveries are made. Put yourself in their shoes and look for their motivation. As you internalize this, you will have a greater understanding as to why they do what they do. By having this perspective and insight, it will be easier for you to provide a more thorough solution for them and will also assist in building your relationship.

The Power of Listening.
Active listening is an art that most can improve on. We listen to people every day and should be very good at it by now. Unfortunately, often we hear only part of what is being said because we aren't paying full attention. I believe that we "hear" things all day long, but most of the time we do not actually "listen."

Listening is an action. This means that we physically do something along with processing what our ears are hearing. We listen with our eyes, our bodies, and our mind in unison. Listening is most effective when our eyes are locked on the person speaking, our bodies are faced towards them, and our minds are open to what is being conveyed. During this process, our sole focus should be on that person, and not anywhere else: not on our phones, or a magazine, or looking off in to the sunset. These are distractions and are taking away from the connection of the conversation.

We should also realize that different people have different needs from their listening audience. Once you realize that, this can help lead to more efficient communication for all involved. For example, my wife and I share two businesses, a household, and two children, amongst many other things. I have learned through trial and much error that whenever we are having an important conversation, I need to be right in front of her and provide my undivided attention. If I am doing anything else at the same time, she becomes distracted, and that takes away from the conversation. To be most effective in our conversations, we need to sit across from each other, lock eyes, and not have any other distractions. This works best for us.

True listening is being open and present to the person speaking so we can learn, grow, and internalize the meaning of what is being said. Many times, we only half-listen, all the while leaping ahead mentally to shape our own response or rebuttal. Perhaps we are thinking of guidance to give or a personal story to offer to empathize with the other person. During these times, we are not truly listening. We are not taking in the entirety of what is being conveyed to us.

Listening fully can be very challenging for many people. To fully commit yourself to listening is something that must be practiced. You must apply focus, fight distractions, and give your whole-hearted attention. Through this effort, you are showing the other person that you respect them and their message and are interested in learning about them. You set the stage for open conversation and create the best opportunity for your own success.

Why?

If you have children in your life, you will appreciate the power of their inquisitive minds. Follow any 3 or 5-year-old around for a day and you will see that they are always looking for answers. Constantly with my own two children I hear, "Why, Daddy? Why should I? Why isn't it? Why won't he? Why didn't she? Why? Why? Why?" Asking "Why?" in the right situation can open the floodgates to more information. This works not only for children but for adults as well. Be careful not to overuse this simple question, however, as it can get worn out easily. Some alternatives that can be used are "Can you elaborate on that?" or "Can you tell me more?"

Here are some other questions that can start or add to a meaningful conversation.

- How are you doing this today?
- What do you like best about your current solution?
- How would you describe your perfect scenario, situation, or solution?
- How is this working for you? What does that mean?
- How does this affect your team?
- If failure was not a possible outcome, how would you...
  » Change your solution?
  » Change your business?
  » Modify your schedule?
- What has been the biggest change in your business in the last year?
- How has this affected you? Your team? Your customers?
- Can you describe your top two to three business challenges?
- Where do you see your business in eighteen months? Three years? Five years?
- Where do you see yourself personally in that same time frame?
- Does that vision match your personal goals? Can you elaborate?

- Why? Why? Why?

The main objective in asking questions is to gain information. Choosing to be present in a conversation and applying all of your attention will uncover not only what is said, but also what is implied. As I mentioned earlier, you have two ears and only one mouth. This is a good reminder again to listen twice as much as you speak.

Ask questions that cannot be answered with a simple yes or no response. Ask your audience to elaborate, clarify, explore, and offer more. Then listen. Let them know you are listening with your eyes, your body, and your voice. Nod your head now and then or perhaps add a vocal "um–hum" or "yes, I understand." Give them permission to continue to give you more information. Seek to understand them and identify and empathize with their position and needs. Be interested and search for the complete story. This will give you knowledge and a foundation that you can build upon.

takeaways & key ideas

1. Learning comes from inquiry.
2. Conversations create relationships.
3. Never underestimate the power of a smile, handshake, and eye contact.
4. Seek to understand others: not just what they do, but why they do it.
5. You were given two ears and one mouth on purpose. Use them with that ratio in mind. Speak less, listen more.
6. Listening is a verb. Do it actively.
7. There is power in the questions that you ask.
8. Dig deeper. Ask "Why?"

considerations

1. How can I modify or revise my line of questioning to learn more from my customer interactions?
2. How can I set the stage for a deeper conversation?
3. During my last discovery session or customer engagement,

what questions could I have asked that I didn't?
4. Do I listen actively at work? Do I listen actively at home? Do I give my full attention during conversations?
5. Do I talk more than I listen?
6. How often do I dig deeper in conversations and ask "Why"?

COMMUNICATION AND FOLLOW-UP

Communication in sales and business is as important as the solution or service itself. Without a proper understanding of things and a constant agreement and alignment amongst all involved parties, the train can go off the tracks quickly. Clear and concise communication is another attribute that typically separates the highest achievers from everyone else. These communications can come in various forms, including in-person meetings, phone interactions, emails, text, follow-ups, meeting notes, letters, and reports. As there are so many avenues to connect with your clients and co-workers, you will have many opportunities to interact successfully and effectively. Unfortunately, this creates many different opportunities to not communicate clearly as well. So how do you ensure that your point is getting across effectively, clearly, and professionally? I will show you how in the pages to come.

Communication involves more than one person.
When we communicate, we are exchanging thoughts, beliefs, or information with someone else. The act of communicating cannot exist without another party or person. This two-way interaction requires active listening that sets the stage for effectively exchanging information—and displays your interest and

respect. These items are necessary for a successful interaction.

Write down everything.

Take notes upon notes upon notes. Record these notes during client meetings, internal team meetings, one-on-ones with your management, and any other time you think it might be helpful." Note-taking during important conversations ensures that topic details and important areas of emphasis are recorded for later review. This practice enables you to have a back-up log, other than your memory, of all events as they transpire. This also shows the other party that you are interested in what is being said enough to record it. This gives them permission to elaborate more on the given topic.

Communication is as important in the sales environment as the solution or service itself.

Communicate with intention.

Communicate with the intention to understand and find agreement. Conversations are best when there is true back-and-forth between parties. This gives everyone the opportunity to offer their perspective and ask for clarity or consideration in order to come to a mutual understanding. There is nothing worse than a one-sided conversation, which are nothing more than orders given, or commands stated. There is no desire for input, agreement, or mutual interaction. If you are a drill sergeant, then this is appropriate. If you want to be successful in business or your personal life, then it is best to create an environment where all involved can contribute until agreement is achieved.

Restate the obvious for clarity and agreement.

One of the most effective practices that I have found when communicating involves restating the obvious or anything that could be "assumed." Assumptions are dangerous; they can sabotage a business or personal relationship. A good way to combat this is by simply saying, "I cannot assume that we are in agreement on this unless we talk about it, so ..." or "I cannot assume that you know this unless we discuss it directly, so...." I also may say, "Please forgive me for restating something that you already know or that seems obvious, but I want to make sure that we have clarity on this." By starting with this approach, you are not only reaffirming a shared understanding of a situation—you are setting the stage for identifying any potential areas of misunderstanding. Either way, you are ensuring that all are on the same page.

Using email to communicate.

Email is a necessary tool in most settings today, so it is essential to use it effectively and appropriately. Emails are unique in that they can be forwarded, responded to, attached to other emails, and brought up at any time in the future to be reviewed or reread. With this enhanced visibility and access, it is important to practice good email habits. Below are six rules that can serve as your guidelines when you send email.

Email Rule #1.

Always reread your email two times before sending. If your email is worth sending, then make sure that you are communicating the best points. Look for structure, spelling, language use, and appropriate style. Once you send that email out, you cannot take it back. Additionally, the person you sent it to will always have a copy. Make sure that you are saying exactly what you want to. Double-check it!

THE **6 RULES** OF EMAIL USAGE

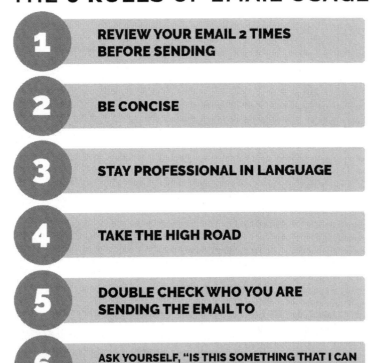

1. **REVIEW YOUR EMAIL 2 TIMES BEFORE SENDING**

2. **BE CONCISE**

3. **STAY PROFESSIONAL IN LANGUAGE**

4. **TAKE THE HIGH ROAD**

5. **DOUBLE CHECK WHO YOU ARE SENDING THE EMAIL TO**

6. **ASK YOURSELF, "IS THIS SOMETHING THAT I CAN ADDRESS IN PERSON OR ON THE PHONE?"**

Email Rule #2.

Be concise. Most people get too many emails and do not have the time to review each and every one. Try to get your point across quickly and use bullet points when appropriate.

Your audience will appreciate it!

Email Rule #3.
Stay professional in language. Do not use slang in emails. Leave this for your conversation in person, if appropriate. Often, misguided attempts at humor or sarcasm can be misinterpreted. Most times slang does not translate well in a written format. Just refrain.

Email Rule #4.
Take the high road. Do not let your emotions get the best of you in an email. Stay professional and leave any rebuttals for an in-person meeting. You will undoubtedly receive a scathing email at some point in your career that you will want to reply to immediately with a quick tongue and a few choice words. Have strength, take a breath, and think about how best to reply. Sometimes in this situation, I like to open a new email (without an address in the "To" field) and write out exactly what I am thinking. This is cathartic and helps me process my thoughts and emotions. Then I will delete the text and start over with how I can professionally respond.

As a reminder, seek to understand. What prompted the sender to write that email? How can you respond and be of service to them? When can you meet with them or talk directly to address their issue? This can all be done outside of a written email.

Email Rule #5.
Double-check who you are sending the email to. There is nothing worse than sending an email to the wrong person, especially if there is sensitive information in that email. Once

you press, "Send," there is no taking it back. Be sure of who it is going to.

Email Rule #6.

Before writing the email, ask yourself, "Is this something that I can address in person or on the phone?" Email has become a crutch for most professionals. Many times, a simple phone call or visit to someone's office is more effective and appropriate. If you find yourself volleying emails back and forth with someone, pick up the phone or get up from behind your desk and seek them out. You may be surprised with how effective this practice is.

There are many other nuances to writing emails. In my corporate career, I sent and received hundreds of emails daily, and I became well-versed on how to respond quickly and effectively. I also learned when not to respond and pick up the phone instead. Think twice before sending—you will thank me later.

Using Text Messages.

Today most everyone has a smartphone or a device that can send and receive text messages. This has made the use of text messages commonplace in both personal and professional settings, although I think that texts are more appropriate for personal communications than business ones. Text messages can be useful at times but should be used with caution in business. The mere nature of a text message, with its limitations on size and the routine use of slang, acronyms, and emojis, does not translate well to the business world. I would stay away from text messaging if possible, although there may be exceptions to the rule at times. For example, if I am running late for a meeting, then I may text ahead and let the other person know that I will be there fifteen minutes after the scheduled start time. Also, I have had times in my career where a customer with whom I was working would respond immediately to a text message when an email or phone call would go unanswered. In those situations, I would use text as a confirmation of meeting or appointment times so that we could then work together in person. Text messaging may become more frequently used in business in the future, but for now, leave it to your personal conversations.

Follow-ups.
An incredibly useful habit to adopt is the practice of following up with others after important meetings or phone conversations. This recap, typically sent via email, can offer a review of all important elements and mutual agreements that were made during the meeting. This process does not have to be over-thought. It should be a short and concise written communication that includes the events that transpired, the agreements that were made, and the next action steps being planned. Even if this seems like overkill, it is necessary. This confirmation will put the exclamation mark on an agreement. This reminder may clear up any misunderstanding or doubt that was left open at the end of a meeting. Additionally, this is a written confirmation of a summary of the events that can be useful at a future date when there may be confusion about what has previously occurred.

The follow-up itself can be in bullet points and simply restate the highlights of the event. It can start with, "Hello Mr. Customer, it was great meeting with you today! I wanted to send along a recap of our meeting notes and propose a time for our next meeting." After that, list the highlights in bullet points and offer a time and date for your next interaction. At the end of the email, include something like, "Please let me know if any of these items need more clarity or if I missed anything." After a long meeting where many things may have been discussed or reviewed, most people will appreciate an abbreviated follow-up that they can refer to as well. Offer recaps after customer meetings, internal team meetings, and any relevant phone calls.

Verbal recap before the written recap.
A tip that will help you create an effective review is to offer a verbal recap at the end of each meeting. During this time, you can end a meeting with, "Thank you for your time today. I would like to take a minute and recap the highlights from today's meeting and review our action items moving forward." This offers agreement and clarity at the close of a meeting and will include the same content that you offer in your written recap. Once again, as clarity is the main goal here, this practice will pay off in the long run.

To reach a level of consistent success, strive to be a master communicator. Don't just listen to what a person says in words; strive to uncover the often-implied message hiding behind those words. Go above and beyond to "over-communicate." Take it as your personal mission to create an environment of mutual understanding. Seek to understand motives and perspectives. Be a "student of the game," and try to learn about how people from all walks of life communicate. Anything you learn will add to your skillset and will undoubtedly contribute to your success.

takeaways & key ideas

1. Clear and concise communication is essential to your success.
2. Create the habit of taking notes all the time. This may save your tail down the road.
3. Restate the obvious for confirmation and agreement. If I assume then it may make an "Ass" out of "U" and "Me."
4. Email is an incredible tool to communicate, but it sometimes is your worst enemy. Take it seriously and use email appropriately.
5. Text messages are for the weekends with your friends. Keep them there.
6. Write follow-up emails after each meeting. It will set you apart from others and will add to your overall efficiency. Sometimes the best emails are the ones not sent. They are replaced with a conversation.
7. Sometimes the best emails are the ones not sent.

considerations

1. How are my communication habits today?
2. How do others perceive my communication skills?
3. What can I change about the way that I typically communicate?
4. Do I write clear, concise, and effective emails?
5. When was the last time that I sent an email when I should have had a conversation instead?
6. When was the last time that I assumed something that got me in trouble? How could I have avoided this?
7. How often do I create written follow up recaps after meetings?

part 4

CREATING YOUR MINDSET FOR ULTIMATE SUCCESS

MIMIC THE OVERACHIEVERS

Author, businessman, and success coach Tony Robbins is quoted as saying, "If you want to be successful, find someone who has achieved the results you want and copy what they do, and you'll achieve the same results." This makes sense, wouldn't you agree? If you think about it, most goals that people set for themselves have already been achieved by someone else. So why wouldn't you want to seek them out to ask them how they have done it? If you want to be a millionaire, go find a millionaire and interview them. If you want to become a CEO, go find a CEO and ask them what they did to get there. If you have always wanted to own a coffee shop, go to your local coffee shop and ask the owner to tell you about their journey for thirty minutes. If you want to run a marathon, first go find someone who has done it and ask them how they trained and prepared for the big event.

If you take this approach, you will learn that most people want to share their story with you. People like to talk about themselves, so asking someone to take a moment to fill you in on their genius generally will produce a wealth of information. You can also find multiple people to interview so that you have a better foundation of information. Remember, the best information stems from the best questions, so plan what you will ask, and record every answer. Thank them also for their time and guidance and follow up with a hand-written thank you card. This information is priceless and will save you time, money, and frustration down the road.

As I mentioned in Chapter 3, when starting my career with Micros, I went through many internal meetings to gain insight on how to do my job best. I interviewed department heads to understand what their goals were and asked each one how my work could best complement theirs. I also asked them the following question: "If you think back over your time here, who was the most successful person who ever had my position? What do you think made them so successful?" This gave me an abundance of information and perspective on the top performers from their peers and co-workers. After I had identified who these people were, I called each of them directly and asked for time with them. During that time, I picked their brains on what had and had not worked for them. I asked them for insights about what they had learned over the course of their careers. By spending this time together, I also set the stage for open communication in the future so that I had a source for further guidance.

I searched for answers from my local team leaders and reviewed top performers in the country. I researched these top reps and their habits and made it a goal to connect with each one. Nearly six months into my first year, our company hosted a sales conference with all reps from around the country. I contacted each of the top five prior to the conference and invited them to coffee, lunch, dinner, or cocktail meetings during our conference. This gave me the ability to spend quality time with them and enabled me to learn from the most successful people in my position. This initial connection helped to create a line of communication that I utilized for years to come. These resources became my most important tools for success as I made my way to becoming the top sales person in the company.

The moral of the story is, don't re-invent the wheel. Find someone who has done what you are trying to do and ask them how they did it. If you are breaking new ground and there is truly no one who has done something that you are attempting, then find someone who has accomplished a similar type of goal in another field. Look for alignments in thought and action. Steal knowledge from other's successes as well as from other's mistakes. Always seek to learn more, and remember, after setting each new goal, ask yourself, "Who has done this before, and how did they do it?"

takeaways & key ideas

1. For most goals, there is someone out there who has achieved it already. Go ask them how they did it.
2. Most people love to share their personal story of success. Capitalize on this.
3. By studying other's successes and mistakes, you will save yourself time and energy, and get to your own success sooner.
4. Thank people for sharing their story and time with you. This will encourage them to do it again in the future.

considerations

1. What three goals do you have that you know others have achieved already? Who has achieved them? Can you ask them to share their story with you?
2. What is one main challenge in business that you get stuck on regularly? Who has figured out how to get past this?
3. Who has a relationship that you admire? Can you ask them to share with you how they maintain this successfully?

WORK/LIFE COUNTER BALANCE

By this time, you have the foundation of sales success laid out in front of you. You know the benefits of building your sales environment by leaning on your team and on the internal resources that are available to you. I have reviewed the importance of setting goals and having a clear vision of what you aim to do and where you plan to go. You understand how to approach your market and dissect it so that you can recognize maximum results. You know the importance of becoming an expert in your field so that you can be of service to those you work with. You have gained insight on each step of the sales cycle and know how to use this process to move customers from introduction through to the close. You have been reminded of the significance of the 4 Rs, and how strong relationships can create success.

I have also covered in depth the importance of tools that you will use along the way, including specific types of technology that can complement your objectives. You know how to manage your time now more thoroughly to ensure that you are using it in the most productive and effective way possible. I have also addressed how to excel in your communication skills and position your line of questioning to create the best opportunity to learn.

Finally, we have taken a step back and reviewed from a high level how to manage your business by defining that the most important activities (your 20%) should receive the majority of your attention (80%).

All of this is assisted when you capitalize on what you can learn from others who have already succeeded, and failed, in doing what you are attempting to do.

The combination of all of these efforts will open the doors of opportunity for you. You now have the fundamentals to be as successful as you want to be. You have the power of knowledge, and this, married to diligent implementation and application, can create unparalleled success.

At this time, it would be very easy for you to throw yourself into your work and apply all that you have learned here. But don't expect results overnight. To be successful in sales and business, you need to work your butt off for some time before recognizing the fruits of your labor. You will need to put in long hours to build your funnel, your relationships, and your market presence. This does not happen overnight. In fact, for most this can take years to build, and these efforts can be all-consuming. But beware: when you have your head down and you are hard at work, it is easy to ignore everything else around you. This is where a lot of people get in to trouble. You see, great success can come at a great cost if you are not careful, and a balance is needed.

Maintaining this balance creates many opportunities. It

affords a chance to recharge yourself to ensure that you do not burn out from too much work. It allows the opportunity to refresh your relationships with those around you. It provides a break to gain a new perspective when reentering your workflow. It also maintains your sanity and gives you the best opportunity for *long-term* success.

Now, as with anything, there is an ebb and flow here. This balance is not an even 50/50. There will be times when you are devoting more time and attention to your work, and other times when your personal life gets more time and devotion. Both aspects of your life have merit and importance, and both will attempt to occupy all of your time if you let them. The best way to manage this relationship is to ensure that each is given appropriate time and nurturing. If you ignore this, and provide only one part of your life nourishment, the other suffers.

So how do you create this balance? How do you ensure that you can succeed in your business and personal life at the same time? Let me share how a lack of balance affected me along my journey and offer some tips to help you find and maintain balance in your life.

> *Great success can come at a great cost if you are not careful—balance is needed.*

In early 2006, there were several life-changing events happening in my family. First, I had just begun my career at Micros.

This was a new industry for me, and although it was not my first position in sales, it seemed quite foreign, as I was only vaguely familiar with the hospitality industry. Second, my wife Julia was just starting a new business, a youth performing arts company that was her area of expertise and training. Third, we were welcoming our first child, Jonah. Like any first-time parent, I had no idea how much my life would change with a new child in our home. These events all happened in the same year and created a world of change. I truly did not realize how much attention that each one would take to become successful—and remain successful.

At Micros, it took about eighteen months before I began to recognize success and find my groove. I felt that I needed to be successful so that I could have the finances to support my new growing family as well as assist Julia's company as she built it. I worked my tail off, making sure that I was the first one to the office and the last one to leave. I was logging 10 to 12-hour workdays daily and picked up the habit of bringing my work home with me. My initial success from all this effort fueled me to work harder as I wanted to be the best of the best. The success was somewhat seductive. Newly-found respect, large paychecks, and more opportunity came along with it. I also had a local territory and declined promotions, as I did not want to travel out of state regularly. I felt that this was a concession that I was making for my family as this would ensure that I was not away on long work trips and could help more at home. What I failed to see was that, although I was not travelling out of state, I was working so much that I was not helpful at home, and when I was there I was too tired to help. I created an environment where Julia was taking care of our child while creating her new business at the same time.

Although my business was growing, my personal relationships were suffering, and something needed to change. Unfortunately, realization would not come until years later.

Over the next few years, my business continued to grow, and concurrently, Julia's business was taking off as well. Although she had brought on additional staff, she was still submerged in the growth and development of the day-to-day business. Nearly three years after starting, Julia became pregnant with our second child, Jett. In addition, we decided that it was time to purchase our first home as well. So now we had two children, two businesses, and a new home. Talk about pressure!

As time went on, both of our businesses grew, and I accepted a promotion as director of sales. I thought that for my long-term success it was the best move to make. My new position included some travel that put me on the road every other week for a few days at a time. This only added to the stress at home as Julia's business had grown exponentially and our children's schedule became more demanding as well. But we carried on.

By 2013, my business at Micros had never been better and my paychecks had never been larger. Julia's business had grown to be the largest of its kind in our area, and we decided to take on a second studio business with a long-term lease. Again, I thought that the decisions we were making were in the best interest of our family unit, but I failed to see the true impact it was having on the happiness of our family and my relationship with Julia.

My failure to see the warning signs created a tipping point that caused a world of grief at home. Consequently, I put on the breaks and reevaluated all areas of my life, with the end goal being to realign myself with my personal and family's goals. Julia and I spent a great deal of time sharing together and defined what our family goals over the next five and ten years would be. It was at that point that I started to create my exit strategy from corporate America and devise a plan for the future. My main focus was on making choices in my business life that would lead to the kind of family and personal life that Julia and I wanted to live. Most importantly, I wanted to apply my time to the things that I desired, and ultimately find more fulfillment.

Today, my life is more balanced than ever before. I "graduated" from corporate America in late 2015 and now work full-time managing our existing businesses. I also am a certified success coach, speaker, and business consultant, and work with clients on finding more fulfillment and success in their lives. I have arranged my schedule to include a healthy daily balance of work, personal, and family time. Work time includes writing, managing my businesses, and new business development. Personal time includes meditation, exercise, and other personal development activities. Family time is spent with Julia, Jonah, and Jett, and also includes time with our extended family and friends.

Each of these areas show up on my calendar to ensure that they actually happen. A large majority of these are also attached to my list of goals. For example, one of my goals is to maintain an incredible relationship with Julia. For me, this is defined as spending regular time together, going on adventures, being romantic, communicating, and connecting spiritually on a weekly basis. These "dates" are on my calendar, regularly, and for us, this creates a balance that nourishes our relationship.

My recommendation for you is first to review your list of goals. Earlier in the book (Chapter 5), we looked at guidelines to help you set goals in business. Here I would utilize that same methodology to include a wider reach to encompass all areas of your life. As a reminder, I recommend that you create goals in each of the seven main areas.

- Financial (income, investments)
- Business (profession, job and career)
- Relationships (family, friends, romance)
- Health and fitness
- Fun time and recreation
- Personal (possessions, education, personal development)
- Contribution and Legacy (service to others)

Now that you have created goals in all of these areas, your next task is to allocate time regularly to each. This practice will create the best opportunity for balance in your life. As stated earlier, you may find that some items take more time, or maybe you simply want to apply your time to some items most often. This is fine. The main objective is to review your activity regularly. Take time to pause and check in with yourself. Are you nourishing your relationships regularly? Are you taking time to develop yourself? Do you have a routine of allowing yourself to disconnect and recharge?

Remember, to achieve at the highest level, you need to be your best self—and to create your best self, there needs to be balance. There is no point working so hard for something in business to have everything else fall apart around you. I have watched many business people climb to the top of their field, only to find themselves alone when they get there. They have sacrificed their marriages, relationships, health, and sanity to get where they are. Most often they cannot tell you exactly where they went off course, but they can certainly tell you that they did. Balance is the key ingredient to creating the life and success you want, and balance gives you the ability to be present and enjoy it daily.

takeaways & key ideas

1. Great success can come at a great cost if you are not careful.
2. Balance is needed to make sure that you are able to give your best to whatever you are doing at that time.
3. Balance is not always 50/50. Be flexible. What may be a 70/30 split one day might be a 20/80 split the next. Look at your weekly and monthly schedule and strive to hit that 50/50 mark overall.
4. Remember to pick your head up at times, pause, and take stock of your life to ensure that you are maintaining a balance.
5. Allocating time on the goals set in the seven main areas helps to ensure that you are maintaining balance.

considerations

1. Would you consider your life today to have balance? If not, how can you change this?

2. Are you spending time nourishing your business relation-ships? Your personal relationships?
3. While developing your business, are you working on de-veloping your mind? Your spirit? Your mental health? Your body?
4. What percentage of your activity and efforts benefit you versus others? Is there a healthy balance?
5. If you imagine your most successful self, what does that look like in your business? In your personal life? In your travel? In service to others? In your material things? In your relationships?
6. Does your calendar today have time blocks scheduled to support these goals? If not, what can you do right now to change this?

CELEBRATE AND STAY POSITIVE

In today's environment of non-ending work, it is becoming ever more important to stop and celebrate our successes. Celebrate what you and others have accomplished and bring attention to the things that people do *right*, not *wrong*. Focus on the positive, not the negative. Now, I know that this is not the norm. In fact, our society has grown accustomed to highlighting the faults and misdoings of people every day. Just take a look at the news. The media highlights negative story after negative story, only to end their broadcast with one "feel-good" piece. How would the news look and feel different if this was reversed? How would the audience feel if every story was of a positive nature? How would it affect people if they only reported stories about people doing the right thing?

I had an epiphany a few years ago as I was thinking about this topic while coaching my son's basketball team. Being a life-long basketball player myself, I was raised on hard, tough-love coaching—men yelling and screaming at me with instructions of criticism and instruction on things *not to do*. They would use negative reinforcement like, "Don't let him beat you"! or "Why didn't you pass?" or "You shouldn't have shot that ball!" I had played basketball all my life and never realized how negative the coaching was. I began to listen to other coaches in youth sports. I noticed a trend in every sport being played. Most coaching from the sidelines was negative.

As an exercise, I started coaching from a positive perspective. I didn't say anything negative, but rather shaped my feedback to motivate the players to think about alternative actions. Instead of, "Why didn't you pass?" I asked, *"What would have happened if you had passed to your teammate instead?"* In place of, *"Don't let him beat you!"* I offered, "What could you do differently to get ahead of him next time?" I found myself offering more compliments during the game on the things they did right, rather than wrong, and their overall play improved.

If we take this one step further, I propose that in most daily conversations, if you pay attention, you will notice a lot of negativity in comments. This often takes the form of a complaint of some sort. This complaint may stem from someone who is taking on a role of a victim. I would suggest conducting an experiment in your own life for a day or two. Take notice of how many times you are in a conversation and a negative or victimizing comment arises. Record how many negative words are used, such as *can't, won't,* or *shouldn't*. Notice the adjectives that are used by many to describe things. Are they positive and complimenting? Are they negative and limiting? Is there an alternative way to convey what is being said? Rather than saying, "That food was disgusting," could you say, "I'm really looking forward to an amazing dinner." This may seem like a small change, but added up it can improve the tone of an entire conversation.

My mentor and friend Jack Canfield teaches that what you

think and say out loud is a prescription that you are asking life to fill. For example, if I tell everyone that I can't find time to get anything done, then truly I will never feel as if I have sufficient time to do anything. Or, if I think, "I'm too fat to ever get a girlfriend," then most likely I won't find one as my thoughts are controlling my actions. The point is that your words and thoughts have power. They have the power to affect not only you, but those around you.

So how does this apply to sales and business? Simple. Stay positive and positivity will follow. Stay focused on what's good and not what's bad. Give people compliments and reward them for doing not just the big things, but also for doing the small things. Give people the credit they deserve. I'm sure that you will surprise them by doing so. Here are some suggestions.

- Highlight a co-worker's accomplishment during a meeting.
- Hand-write a thank you card.
- Bring a cup of coffee in for someone.
- Offer to take someone to lunch.
- Give a gift card for a movie.
- Ask a customer to write a letter of recommendation for an associate.
- Let someone take the rest of the day off.
- Say "Thank you!" (a lot).

Remember, businesses are built on relationships, and people like to have relationships with positive people. Positive energy creates and stimulates further positive energy. Now I know that everything will not be rosy all the time, but a conscious effort to stay positive and stay above the negativity will have an incredible effect on your business. Trust me, this can change the game. Also, take it one step further and apply it to all areas of your life. You will notice the impact immediately and making it a habit will change your life.

takeaways & key ideas

1. Start your team meetings with a "What's good?" session. This starts your meeting on a positive note and sets a tone for the meeting.
2. Positive thoughts produce many benefits, including higher energy levels, greater optimism, healthier lifestyles, better sleep, and stronger relationships.
3. Being positive draws other positive people to you.
4. When you set a goal, set an associated reward that you will get along with it.
5. Make sure to celebrate your success and the success of others.

considerations

1. Would you consider yourself a positive person? Do you show this in your actions, conversations, and daily life?
2. What is the last business success that you achieved? How did you celebrate this? If you didn't, how can you celebrate

it now?

3. What business / personal goal have you set to achieve in the next thirty days? What do you have planned to celebrate your victory?
4. When was the last time you celebrated someone else's achievement? How did you celebrate this? How can you do this again for others?
5. Is the language you use daily positive? If not, how can this change?

THE POWER OF GRATITUDE

Gratitude is a superpower that many people do not realize they have. The practice of being grateful creates an abundance of beneficial things for you in your life if used regularly. Being grateful creates a mindset that is positive. In the last chapter, we discussed the advantages that being positive can have in your life. As a reminder, positive people, more often than others, experience higher energy levels, greater optimism, more healthy lifestyles, better sleep, and stronger relationships.

Practicing gratitude regularly will help to attract more positivity to your life also. The law of attraction tells us that what you choose to keep at the top of mind and focus on regularly will appear more regularly in your life. When you focus on something, you are telling the universe to bring more of it to your life. This concentrated attention will assist with programming your brain to look for more of it every day. It will help you apply logic and problem-solving skills to ensure that you can experience more of what you are grateful for.

The practice of being grateful can come through meditation or a daily ritual such as a writing in a gratitude journal. The goal is to either contemplate or write down all the things for which you are grateful. These can be simple things like the food you eat, the air you breathe, or the flowers in your backyard. They can be bigger things, such as your home, your relationship with your partner, or the success that you have achieved in your business. Regardless of what you are thankful for, the practice of pausing to recognize those things is the objective.

In my life, I have created a daily routine where I start my day with a gratitude exercise. I think of five things that I am grateful for and why I am grateful for them. At the end of the day, I follow the same exercise and think about things that I am grateful for that affected me that day. Sometimes I write these down in my journal. Other times I merely just go through the exercise in thought. I also try to consciously thank as many people as possible through the day. It could be a short thank you to the clerk at the gas station, the parking valet, the host at a restaurant, or a parent at the studio. I find that looking someone in the eyes, offering a smile, and saying thank you is quite therapeutic for me. Try it and see if you feel the same way.

Another exercise to try would be a gratitude walk. With this exercise, I head out my front door and walk around the block. I take notice of the things around me that I take for granted constantly. I am grateful for the sidewalk that was built for me to walk along. I am grateful for the trees on my street adding oxygen to the air and offering color and shade. I appreciate the power lines as they carry power to my home so that I can turn the lights on and use my appliances whenever I chose to. I appreciate the nicely-paved streets that have been created and maintained by the public works department. I appreciate the gutters in the street that carry the excess rainwater from the streets to avoid flooding. And so on, and so on. The point of this exercise is to create a habit of gratitude. You will most likely find that this will then move to other areas throughout the day and into your interactions with people.

Have you ever thanked a grocery store employee for working on a holiday? If you think about it, they may like to be home with their family, too. Instead, they are working and available to help you get your last-minute necessities for your holiday celebration. I try to make it a habit to tell them how much I appreciate what they do so that I can be prepared to celebrate. This typically makes someone's day, and it is so easy to do.

Living in Service.
Having gratitude and being thankful go hand-in-hand with living in service. When you live in service, you do your best to make sure that every interaction helps another person in some way. Your intention is true, and your objective is to create benefits for all involved. You are grateful and thankful for the opportunity to connect and assist. This creates harmony and lends to creating your best and most complete self.

This is so important in business and applies to sales specifically. You see, when your integrity and intentions are combined with your willingness to assist and offer solutions, success will come in abundance. This has been proven time and time again, in every position, in every industry, and in every country around the world. This theory transcends all else and combined with the sales strategies which we have covered in this book, create an ideal foundation to build upon.

takeaways & key ideas

1. Gratitude improves your health, relationships, emotions, personality, and career.
2. Gratitude makes you less self-centered and enables you to focus on being of service to others.
3. Gratitude makes you a more effective manager and co-worker.
4. Being grateful is a state of mind. You either decide to be grateful or not.

considerations

1. Do you have a lot of things in your life to be grateful for? (rhetorical question) How often do you think about how lucky you are?
2. How often do you thank others for exceeding expectations?
3. How often do you thank others for doing simple things?
4. Can you write out five things that you are grateful for every day for the next seven days? Will you share them with

someone else? Who will you share them with? When will you do this?

5. Who can you include in a gratitude circle or conversation? What benefits could you introduce to someone else through this action?

FINAL THOUGHTS AND OTHER TIDBITS

Tim Ferriss, in his latest book release *Tools of Titans*, interviews billionaires, icons, and world-class performers to learn the tactics, routines, and habits that have catapulted them to success. A recurring trend amongst a majority of them is that they have a daily morning routine that sets them up for a successful day. Here are the things that are generally spoken of in regard to a daily morning routine.

Consistent early wake-up time.
High-achievers typically wake up early. They start their day before others and arise with energy ready to take on the world. As they say, "The early bird gets the worm."

Meditation.
Meditation, or some form of mindful moment, is part of a typical routine as it starts the day with creating inner focus and peace. High achievers find that even minutes of meditation can help to center them and create balance for the day. Meditation starters can check out www.calm.com for a free meditation track or search for guided or unguided meditation on YouTube where you will find hundreds of options. The goal here is to pause and direct your attention inwards so that you

can strengthen your mind and create peace as a foundation for your day. Try it for seven days and it can change your life.

Gratitude.
As covered in the last chapter, gratitude is a secret weapon that we all possess that can add multiple benefits to our day. Start your day with a similar exercise referenced previously where you write down or think about five things you are grateful for. Do the same at night.

Exercise.
Regardless of where you are or what role you play in your world, find time to exercise. Don't think you have time? Wake up earlier and walk or stretch. Can't make it out of the hotel room? No problem. Do some push-ups and sit-ups, or search for a yoga session on YouTube. Exercise raises your heart rate and stimulates physical and mental energy. It kick-starts your metabolism and creates a routine that can help you maintain your fitness goals. This also will lead to a more productive day and better sleep at night.

Personal Development.
Add ten minutes of personal development reading or audio to your morning. (If you would like to see a portion of my personal reading list, visit www.captureyourpower.com/resources.) Find something that motivates you and stimulates thought. Give your mind a chance to explore something that is not related to work or your daily tasks. If you've ever heard the phrase, "Garbage in, garbage out," then you know that what you digest will find a way to express itself at some point. Make sure that you "digest" something positive, uplifting, and thought-provoking. When it comes out it will add to your

life's experience.

Healthy Meal.
Within the first hour of waking, eat something healthy. Some people do not like to eat breakfast, but there are many studies that prove that eating something in the first hour after waking will kick-start your metabolism and program your body for the day ahead. This can be a snack or a full breakfast, but most importantly, make it something healthy. If you are like most, you will undoubtedly eat some crap at some point during the day. Don't let it be breakfast. Start with something healthy and push the sugar and fat to a later time. Give yourself this one win in the morning and you will feel the effects. Additionally, throughout the day, be mindful of what you eat. My friend and colleague Chris Oden (who has 3% body fat), used to tell me, "Most people are not mindful when they are eating. Just look at what you are about to put in your mouth and ask yourself if you should really be eating this. If the answer is no, then find something else to eat." Words to live by.

Plan for the Day.
Jack Canfield talks often about what he calls his "Hour of Power" that includes a combination of meditation (20 minutes), exercise (20 minutes), and personal development (20 minutes). I agree that this is a great idea for the first portion of your morning. A plan for the rest of the day is important as well—not just for success in sales and business, but in your everyday life, too. Know what you are doing daily. Write it down; plan your work and work your plan. If you choose to stray from your program, then at least you know what you are straying away from. Remember, planning the night before gives you a kick-start to tackle the next day.

Final Thoughts and Other Tidbits

There is a lot here. What is the best way to start applying what you have learned? There are two schools of thought on this: either dive into the deep end or just put a toe in the shallow end. Both approaches will work; it depends on you and your comfort level. My recommendation is to start with something that you are drawn to. For example, if you have never set goals before, start there. Either set goals in all the areas discussed and write SMART goals for each or start slow and just work on one. Either way, the most important thing to do is start. Whether you dive in fully or just lean in, you are headed in the right direction either way. Once again, starting is the most important thing here.

Writing this book was my breakthrough goal that I set in August of 2015. I had never written a book before and frankly did not know where to start or how to make time to complete it. After I visualized how the book would be structured, I had the task of starting to write. I accomplished this by waking up one hour early, every day, six days a week. I would wake up, make coffee, and sit in front of my computer. Many days, my only accomplishment was checking emails or Facebook. Some days, I would only get ten minutes of writing in, and other days I would get more. But I kept at it. Day after day, even when I wanted to stay in bed, I got up. After six months of this, I completed my book. I definitely leaned in to the process. You see, six months would have passed regardless, but now, I have a book that has been completed. It took effort, but typically anything worth having takes effort. Remember, everything you want is just outside of your comfort zone.

What does it take to be successful?
I was asked this question by a young sales rep many years

ago and have been asked many times since. I answered with a question: "What is your definition of success?" See, my definition of success may not be yours. Some would measure their success by the size of their bank accounts, some by their company's share of the market, and still others by a happy marriage. The first thing to do is to define what success looks like to you. The second thing to do is to realize that this vision will most likely change multiple times over the course of your life. In my twenties, I measured success by the amount of money I had (or didn't have). In my thirties, my definition of success also included "happiness," although I needed to define what happiness meant to me. Today, at the ripe old age of forty-five, I equate success with living intentionally every day, being able to live by my own design, and having an impact on other's lives in a positive way.

> " *The most important thing to do is start. Whether you dive in fully or just lean in, you are headed in the right direction either way.*

No matter what your vision of success is, start with a clear understanding of what it looks like to you. After you have a clear vision, imagine yourself achieving it in full color, with all of your senses present. Imagine how it smells, tastes, sounds, looks, and feels. Once you have this vision at the top of your mind, you will know what you are working towards, and will easily recognize it when it appears.

In Ferriss' book, he shares interviews with leaders in business, medicine, entertainment, government, education, and social awareness. Throughout those interviews, the same characteristics show up over and over again as traits of these accomplished and successful people. These traits include integrity, compassion, honesty, servitude, creativity, risk-taking, transparency, efficiency, goal-oriented, and a desire to learn and grow. Of course, there are many other personality traits to strive for, but the presence of these will propel you to the next level in whatever path you choose to take. Seek to grow, as the mere process of the search will make you more than you are today.

Why did I write this book?
After years of working in sales and executive management for various organizations, I began to see commonalities in people who had greater success than others. I spent my time coaching junior reps and sales teams and found that even very successful sales professionals would attend and be engaged with what I had to say. The nature of the sales fundamental workshops that I held was to introduce to some, and serve as a reminder to others, of what the basics looked like daily. You see, everyone needs fundamentals. Even Kobe Bryant, (my favorite basketball player of all time) showed up every day to his job and worked on the basics. He trained and trained on things that he had done thousands of times in the past. He dribbled and shot from the same spot where he had already made hundreds of shots. He studied video of games after they were done before he played the next opponent. He was always the first one shooting in the gym and the last one to leave. Was he the best because of his talent, or was he the

best because of the work he continued to put in everyday? I say both. Success comes to those who work hard, and then work harder, and then when they make it, work the hardest yet. Never stop working towards what you want, and never stop working even after you get there. Period.

So, I wrote this book to help those who need a blueprint. I wanted to give clues of how to rise to the top. Most professionals who are successful already have figured out the majority of what I have written here. If you are not so lucky to be there yet, then let this serve as your guide. If you only do what is here, then you will be successful. Throw in some luck as well, and you can reach heights you never thought possible.

> *Seek to grow, as the mere process of the search will make you more than you are today.*

What role does motivation, growth mindset, and empowerment play in business today?

Our world is changing. Our ability to conceive new thoughts and emotions is increasing. Our capabilities to do new things and be creative are at an all-time high. We can maintain a grounded sense of self and recognize our impact on this planet while being successful. We can use our work, collectively, to benefit others and ourselves at the same time. This is our win-win.

I'll ask the question: If we can succeed while serving others simultaneously, then shouldn't we? If we can learn and make ourselves better every day, then why wouldn't we want to? In today's world, I believe that there are too many people limiting what they can do.

Greatness, genius, and incredible talent abound. Elevate your mind, seek more knowledge, and believe you can. Once you embrace this, the floodgates of success will open.

What is my wish for you?
My wish for you is that you have learned some new tips and techniques to apply both to your business and in your personal life—tips and techniques that will catapult you to new levels of success. I hope that my stories have entertained you while stimulating new thoughts and perspectives. I would feel successful in this project if it motivated you to learn more, feel more, think more, and be more. My intention has been to assist you not just in sales and business, but in life as well. I pray that you will visualize all that you want, then create goals to make them a reality.

You see, we all have the power to succeed. We all have the power to live a fulfilled life, and we all have the power to create our own happiness. All you need to do is capture your power and apply your focus to what you want. Begin today and create the tomorrow that you've always dreamed of.

To Your Success!

Mark Mirkovich
www.CaptureYourPower.com
Mark@CaptureYourPower.com

ADDITIONAL RESOURCES

For more information on Mark's coaching, both personal and business, to be added to his mailing list, or to download additional resources, please visit

www.CaptureYourPower.com

ABOUT THE AUTHOR

Mark Mirkovich is an expert on creating the best mindset and routines for success in sales and business. As a former sales director for an international Fortune 500 company, he holds a unique first-hand experience in how to lead teams and individuals to recognize their power and capture their success. Mark left corporate America in late 2015 to pursue his passion of helping others find more fulfillment in their lives, both personally and professionally. Today, he is a coach, speaker, consultant, author, and recognized top performer. He resides in Los Angeles with his wife, Julia, and sons, Jonah and Jett.

NEED SALES TRAINING?

Mark works with large and small sales teams and management to assist in defining and clarifying goals and aligning team vision. As you have learned in this book, Mark provides a blueprint for sales and business success!

As Mark was a sales top-producer and team leader himself, he understands the daily challenges and opportunities which present themselves in business. His techniques and style of coaching are sure to enable your organization to recognize increased revenue, increased team morale, and crystalized strategic vision for the future.

Key Areas of Focus include
Creating Top Producers
Building Team Synergy
Relationship Selling
Market Approach
Sales Process Development
Secrets to Goal Setting
Habits of Over-Achievers
Daily Routines for Success
Intentional Selling

For more information, visit www.captureyourpower.com/sales

LOOKING TO HIRE A COACH?

Mark works with individual clients to help them recognize and define their own power. Mark believes that each person holds the power to obtain anything they want. That power can be harnessed to provide success, fulfillment, and the life you've always wanted!

Have you ever wondered "What if?". What if you left that job? What if you asked her out? What if you told him just how you felt? Taking chances, leaning in to change, and stepping through fear is part of capturing all that you deserve. Today is the day to take the leap. Request a free consultation with Mark to discuss the first steps to begin your journey! Capture your power - change your life!

Discover tools which you can use every day to get you from where you are to where you want to be!

Learn how to...
- Take Responsibility for your Life
- Define your life's passion
- Discover how to remove roadblocks and barriers which inhibit your success and happiness
- Utilize goal setting in your everyday life

- Use visualization and affirmation to obtain your dreams
- Feel the fear and do it anyway
- Build and maintain stronger relationships
- Create a design for your life!

For more information on hiring Mark as a coach, visit www.captureyourpower.com/coaching

NEED TEAM BUILDING/ TRUST BUILDING?

Mark introduces team building and trust exercises through creative play and improv. With a background in the cultural arts, Mark taps in to acting, improv, and roll playing to emphasize company directives and organizational objectives. Ask Mark for a customized platform for your team. The experience is unparalleled!

Team cohesion and synergy live at the core of success. Leadership exists at all levels, from the C-Suite to the front line. If cultivated and developed, this leadership can catapult an organization to new heights.

TEAM BUILDING THROUGH CREATIVE PLAY AND IMPROV

Teams will realize...
- Enhanced and renewed trust
- Increased communication skills
- Conflict Resolution practices
- Increased Morale
- How to be a Leader in every position
- Work / Life Counter-Balance
- Process Stress Management

- The Power of Recognition

Through his first-hand experience in executive management and working with organizations over the last 25 years, Mark successfully guides your team through recognizing their power to influence the desired outcome and objectives of the business. Organizations experience increased morale, productivity, and revenue, all while building trust and mutual respect.

For more information, visit
www.captureyourpower.com/team-building

INTERESTED IN A KEYNOTE OR WORKSHOP?

Mark offers workshops designed to assist groups with recognizing and capturing their own power. These workshops are intended to provide tools and techniques which audience members can use daily to enhance their life and capture all that they desire. Workshops are experiential and incredibly impactful, and typically are conducted in 1/2 day, 1 day, or multiple days based upon client objectives. Workshops can be tailored to small groups or large groups. Contact Mark today to inquire about a workshop for your team, your organization, or your small group of friends.

Keynote topic examples (30 minutes - 2 hours)

- Goal Setting and Taking-Action
  » Visualization, Affirmation, Breakthrough Goals vs Process Goals, The Power of Thought
- Success Training
  » Taking 100% Responsibility, Accountability, Cleaning Up Your Messes, Healthy Habits of Everyday Superstars
- Presentation Skills
  » How to Speak Like A Pro, Overcoming Fear and Nerves, Be Prepared, Engaging Your Audience

- Sales / Business Success
  - » Everyone is in Sales, How to Approach Your Market, Habits of Overachievers, Lead with Intention, Living in Gratitude, Trust Building
- Inspirational
  - » Courage to Live, Living Your Passion, Being of Service, Finding Your Voice Amongst the Masses, The Choice of Perspective
- Leadership Development
  - » Values Based Leadership, Communication, Conflict Resolution, Starting with the Why

To customize a keynote for your audience, please contact Mark to discuss your objectives and goals for the event. We are happy to collaborate with you on a unique and impactful message.

For more information,
visit www.captureyourpower.com/workshops-keynotes

NEED TO CHANGE YOUR CORPORATE CULTURE?

In the most ideal working environment, teams would live, share, and thrive with a shared sense of unity and direction. They would feel excitement, engagement, and a synergy of personal and organizational cohesion. They would be empowered with growth and development opportunities, all while enhancing the customer experience. They would have shared values and shared vision, which in turn would create a successful, profitable, and socially conscious organization.

Mark is a certified Cultural Transformation Tools (CTT) practitioner. These tools are one of the most detailed and comprehensive cultural diagnostics and values assessment instruments available to leaders and organizations today. They are designed to support leaders in building high-performance, values-driven cultures that attract and keep talented people and increase staff engagement.

The CTT surveys provide the input you need to plan and manage your:

- Change initiatives
- Cultural transformation programs
- Diversity interventions

- Talent management
- Leadership development initiatives
- Customer feedback

They make the intangibles tangible and provide lead indicators for measuring individual and collective performance.

To schedule a free values assessment today, please visit www.captureyourpower.com/culture

Made in the USA
Columbia, SC
19 September 2018

INTERNET WITH
WINDOWS XP

in easy steps

MARY LOJKINE

t of Computer Step

n

. England

http://www.ineasysteps.com

Notice of Liability

Every effort has been made to ensure that this book contains accurate
and current information. However, Computer Step and the author shall
not be liable for any loss or damage suffered by readers as a result of
any information contained herein.

Trademarks

Microsoft® and Windows® are registered trademarks of Microsoft
Corporation. All other trademarks are acknowledged as belonging to
their respective companies.

Printed and bound in the United Kingdom

ISBN 1-84078-200-5